POMERANIAN

SANDY BERGSTROM MESMER

Pomeranian

Editors: Stephanie Fornino, Matt Haviland, Samantha Marrazzo
Indexer: Dianne L. Schneider
Designer: Angela Stanford
Series Designer: Mary Ann Kahn

TFH Publications®
President/CEO: Glen S. Axelrod
Executive Vice President: Mark E. Johnson
Publisher: Albert Connelly, Jr.
Associate Publisher: Stephanie Fornino

Discovery Communications, Inc. Book Development Team: Marjorie Kaplan, President and General Manager, Animal Planet Media/Patrick Gates, President, Discovery Commerce/Elizabeth Bakacs, Vice President, Creative and Merchandising/Sue Perez-Jackson, Director, Licensing/Bridget Stoyko, Designer

TFH Publications, Inc.®
One TFH Plaza
Third and Union Avenues
Neptune City, NJ 07753

Printed and bound in China

14 15 16 17 18 19   1 3 5 7 9 8 6 4 2

Library of Congress Cataloging-in-Publication Data
Mesmer, Sandy Bergstrom.
  Pomeranian / Sandy Bergstrom Mesmer.
     pages cm
  Includes index.
  ISBN 978-0-7938-4948-2 (alk. paper)
  1. Pomeranian dog. I. Title.
  SF429.P8M47 2014
  636.76--dc23
                              2013044807

This book has been published with the intent to provide accurate and authoritative information in regard to the subject matter within. While every reasonable precaution has been taken in preparation of this book, the author and publisher expressly disclaim responsibility for any errors, omissions, or adverse effects arising from the use or application of the information contained herein. The techniques and suggestions are used at the reader's discretion and are not to be considered a substitute for veterinary care. If you suspect a medical problem consult your veterinarian.

Note: In the interest of concise writing, "he" is used when referring to puppies and dogs unless the text is specifically referring to females or males. "She" is used when referring to people. However, the information contained herein is equally applicable to both sexes.

The Leader In Responsible Animal Care for Over 50 Years!®
www.tfh.com

CENTRAL
Garden & Pet

CONTENTS

ORIGINS OF YOUR POMERANIAN

L oyal, cheerful, and sassy, the Pomeranian looks on life as a joyful romp. This tiny powder puff of a dog might appear like just another piece of arm candy ready to rock the red carpet, but there is a story behind the breed that makes it every inch a real, if miniature, dog. To truly understand your Pom, you need to know his history.

THE STORY BEHIND THE DOG

Dogs developed from wolves. Based on many studies and a large number of skull measurements and examinations of the size and structure of the brain, blood, and numbers of chromosomes, whether Pomeranians, German Shepherd Dogs, or Great Danes, all dogs are descended solely from the wolf. Genetically speaking, a wolf is little more distant from the domestic dog than a wild mustang is to a quarter horse.

Remains confirm that wolves were first domesticated in China about 15,000 years ago. Wolves initially discovered that humans had delectable garbage dumps and got in the habit of hanging out for easy meals. Over many generations, they became more dependent upon their human providers, making the switch from associates to partners and finally to pets. It's easy to look at a Siberian Husky or German Shepherd Dog and think of wolf ancestors, but what about a Pomeranian? How can a 50- to 100-pound (22.5- to 44.5-kg) creature have anything at all to do with the puff ball of a cheerful Pom? Genetics tells the tale, of course, but there is more to the story than just rough facts.

THE HUMAN—DOG RELATIONSHIP

From the beginning, humans and wolves had a synergistic relationship: Wolves helped humans protect their caves and eventually houses, and humans helped the wolves maintain a regular food supply. An initial change from wolf to dog points firmly to the path the Pomeranian would eventually take:
• The smaller wolves needed the humans more than the big ones did.
• The smaller wolves had cuter babies—in other words, the "awwww" factor started right at the beginning of domestication.

So as dogs moved away from being wolves (*Canis lupus*) to dogs (*Canis familiaris*), they got smaller. Small dogs first appeared in the Middle East, and archeological evidence points to the fact that it was here that dogs moved from being humankind's associate to best friend.

DOG VARIETY

But how is it possible that 1 wolf ancestor could have branched out into the 350 to 400 recognized dog breeds we see today? A project called CanMap, a

Over time, dogs became smaller, eventually leading to the cheerful Pom.

collaboration among Cornell University, UCLA, and the National Institutes of Health (NIH), gathered DNA from more than 900 dogs representing 80 breeds as well as wild canids. They discovered that complex differences among breeds such as hair length, ear shape and position, and coat color are determined by only 50 genetic "switches." In all other animals, hundreds of genes interact to produce a physical trait. For dog traits, it's usually three. This solves the age-old puzzle of why canines have become the most diverse animal on the planet.

"The story that is emerging," says Robert Wayne, a biologist at UCLA, "is that diversity in dogs derives from a small genetic tool kit." Genetic selection in dogs is thousands of times easier than in all other animals, which explains how an 85-pound (38.5-kg) Alaskan Malamute and a 3-pound (1.5-kg) Pomeranian can stem from one ancestor.

THE POM'S LINEAGE

Most breeds start out by mixing one breed with another for a specific purpose, then tweaking the outcome until the desired result is achieved and the dogs breed "true" (that is, they reproduce themselves generation after generation).

Not so the Pomeranian. If royalty is achieved through consanguinity, then the Pom is royal indeed. He can trace his lineage straight back to the canine's first ancestor, the wolf. The northern-type breeds (which range from the Malamute to the Akita, the American Eskimo to the Pomeranian) are genetically the closest canine relatives to the wolf, sharing the same basic physical traits like a thick double coat, erect ears, and long plume of a tail.

While there is no trace of "big bad wolf" temperament left in a Pom, they are extremely loyal to their own people. They don't howl but can be pretty chatty, voicing detailed opinions about the neighbor's cat, the length of the grass, and the sun coming up.

What route did the Pomeranian travel to morph from a gray wolf loping along the icy tundra to a tiny ball of fluff waiting eagerly for his human to arrive home?

THE POMERANIAN IN EUROPE

In about 1000 AD, the Vikings in Scandinavia and northern Europe decided that they could have a better life farming than burning and pillaging. A need arose for traders to deliver goods to the various villages along the North Sea and Baltic Ocean. These middlemen worked in boats but really were more merchant than sailor. They needed tough and hardy canine companions to keep them company, but realistically, they needed more buddy than protector. After all, these traders wanted to make friends with the villagers, not intimidate them. So over many generations, they picked the most outgoing, cheerful, and energetic puppies available to be their road companions. The result was a medium-sized dog with a rough coat, erect ears, and a cheerful, happy-go-lucky temperament. The Dutch version of this trader's dog became the Keeshond, whose job was to accompany the barge owners along the many canals of

The Pomeranian morphed from the gray wolf loping along the icy tundra to a tiny ball of fluff waiting eagerly for his human to arrive home.

Holland. The northern European version became the family of "German Spitz" dogs ("spitz" meaning "pointed" in German, perhaps referring to their wedge-shaped muzzles) and came in five sizes, ranging from the Wolf Spitz to the Zwerg (miniature) Spitz. They accompanied their masters along the watery byways of northern Germany and Poland. They watched the boat when their owners went dirt-side to trade or for a pint and were at all times a cheerful and uncomplaining buddy.

KING GEORGE III AND QUEEN CHARLOTTE

Seven hundred years later, in 1767, a lonely 17-year-old bride found herself a long way from her native Mecklenburg, a small duchy on the Baltic Sea. Wanting something to remind her of home, she asked for two of her native Zwerg Spitz dogs. A pair arrived in due course from Mecklenburg's neighbor to the east, Pomerania. These dogs were white, weighed about 30 pounds (13.5 kg), and possessed sweet, cheerful dispositions. Young Queen Charlotte, wife of Great Britain's King George III, was captivated and so was the entire country, especially after the dogs' portrait was painted by the renowned Thomas Gainsborough. The breed, now called Pomeranians after the duchy from which they came, gained in popularity in England.

KING GEORGE IV

King George III's successor, King George IV, kept a Pomeranian or two, but the country waned in its affection for the breed at about the same rate it grew tired of its monarch. George IV had no children, so when he died, his niece Victoria ascended the throne.

QUEEN VICTORIA

That Queen Victoria played a pivotal role in the development of the Pomeranian comes as no surprise. Arguably one of the earliest and certainly one of the most influential catalysts in the popularity of more than 20 breeds, Victoria championed the novel idea that one should love their pets "not wisely, but too well." Ascending the throne as a young woman, she proceeded to preside over her nation for the following 64 years. Under her reign, Britain expanded to the far reaches of the world, from India to South Africa to China. The country experienced an explosion of world influence, coining the phrase "The sun never sets on the Union Jack" (Great Britain's flag), and at the top sat the Empress Victoria. When her husband Albert died at 42, she turned to her beloved dogs for solace. After that, all royal events, no matter how formal, had several of her pets present.

Queen Victoria played a pivotal role in the development of the Pomeranian.

Victoria remained a revered role model for her entire long reign, and her passions invariably became the passions of the nation.

In 1888, Victoria fell in love with a 12-pound (5.5-kg) Pomeranian sprite named Marco she found in Florence while touring the Mediterranean. Marco, as well as several of his female relatives, were acquired by the royal canine connoisseur. Marco was considerably smaller than Queen Charlotte's larger and coarser dogs and a rich orange as opposed to the earlier queen's white-and-cream dogs.

Dog shows were then in their infancy, but Victoria didn't hesitate to put her Poms in competition. "Windsor's Marco" was one of many so exhibited. (As an aside, one can only wonder what it felt like to campaign against one of the queen's dogs!) The shows also brought her Poms in front of the general public, who avidly followed all such events in the press. Over time Poms became smaller and smaller, following Victoria's fancy, and turned from the cream and white preferred by an earlier generation to the Queen's favorite deep orange.

As the Queen lay dying in 1901, one of her last requests that her dear Pom Turi be put on the bed next to her. It is a testament to this cheerful and very loyal breed that Turi snuggled in tightly—one can easily envision the pricked ears and liquid brown eyes resting gently on an arm, watching every labored breath, doing all she can to comfort her dying mistress.

KENNEL CLUB RECOGNITION

Pomeranians were recognized by the Kennel Club in 1870, but none were entered in shows until 1871. They weren't very popular—in the whole of 1890, not a single Pom was shown—and tended to be the larger white or cream version and heavier in bone. When Queen Victoria swept onto the scene, everything changed, and by 1905 there were 125 Pomeranian entries at a single show.

The early English Pomeranian weighed 10 to 12 pounds (4.5 to 5.5 kg) and often more. But breeders moved quickly to reduce the dog's size, and weight was often an animated source of discussion. As the smaller specimens tended to win bench show prizes, eventually the standard was adjusted accordingly. Great care was taken to ensure that even the smaller specimens remained healthy and hardy. Thanks are due to these early breeders for establishing a strong and sturdy base for the current breed.

His smaller size, striking coat, and delightfully cheerful and loyal temperament made the Pomeranian immensely fashionable and popular in the early 1900s.

Poms were shown in the AKC's Miscellaneous Class until 1900, when they were officially recognized.

THE POMERANIAN IN THE US

By the late 1800s, fashionable America looked firmly to England for the latest in stylish chic. Victoria's latest chosen breed did not pass unnoticed in the US. The first Pomeranian to be recognized by the American Kennel Club (AKC) was Dick in 1888, but Poms were shown in the AKC's Miscellaneous Class until 1900, when they were officially recognized. In the same year the American Pomeranian Club was formed, and as breeders swiftly took on the English habits of celebrating various different colors and emphasizing size reduction, the breed quickly gained in popularity.

Famous Pom owners include Liberace and the Ziegfeld Follies girls.

The American Pomeranian Club became a member club of the AKC in 1909 and held its first Specialty show with a respectable entry of 138. Next year they outdid themselves with an entry of 185.

World War I was a boon to American Pom breeders. Before this, Americans naturally turned to England for their stock; with the war this wasn't possible, and breeders this side of the pond fell back on their own devices. Mrs. Vincent Motta became one of the earliest American Pom breeders, and her Dixieland line is visible in many pedigrees today. Ch. Aristic Dear Adorable, bred by Gladys Schoenberg and shown by Mary S. Brewster (both prominent Pom breeders in the 1950s), won multiple group and Best in Show titles. Her great great-grandfather was Mrs. Motta's Ch. Dixieland Shining Gold.

THE POMERANIAN TODAY

In the years before World War II, Mary S. Brewster began to breed Pomeranians under the prefix Robwood. She bred many top-winning dogs over the years and her kennel supplied national contenders for many other fanciers, including today's well-known judge Edd Bivin. He started with Pomeranians at the age of 12 after his parents told him that he could show whatever breed he wished, as long as it was small. Edd chose the Pom because it was a little dog with a big attitude.

No talk of exceptional Pomeranians within the last 25 years is complete without mentioning Ch. Great Elms Prince Charming II, owned by Olga Baker and Skip Piazza and bred by Ruth Beam. The applause was like thunder as this penultimate showman strutted his stuff to the top of the leader board at the Westminster Kennel Club dog show in 1988. He personified a big dog in a compact package, and the loving bond demonstrated between dog and handler left no eye dry.

FAMOUS POMERANIAN OWNERS

So who has owned a Pomeranian? You might be surprised! Marie Antoinette kept several, as did Liberace, Fran Drescher of *The Nanny* fame, Sharon Osbourne, Britney Spears, and several of the Ziegfeld Follies girls. Other Pom aficionados include:

- **Chopin:** Chopin didn't have a Pom of his own, but he enjoyed his friends' dogs so much that he composed the famous "Valse du Petit Chien" (or "Small Dog Waltz") for them, which has since been alternately cheered or cursed by generations of piano students.
- **Emile Zola:** Zola, a friend of many French Impressionists, was painted by several, notably Cezanne and Manet. Maybe his Poms played with Mary Cassatt's cheeky Brussels Griffons? One can only wonder.
- **Michelangelo and Mozart:** Michelangelo had a Pom, and Mozart kept a Pom named Pimperl. Pomeranians love nothing better than to watch their humans—one can just imagine the captivation of these two lucky dogs at the masterpieces flowing from their owners' fingers.
- **Isaac Newton:** Isaac Newton's Pom Diamond caused years' worth of his research papers to be burned. Hopefully not on purpose!
- **Martin Luther:** Even Martin Luther, iconic figure of the Protestant Reformation, had a Pomeranian. As he died in 1546, it's easy to see that this friendly and loyal breed has been around for a very long time.

CHAPTER 2

CHARACTERISTICS OF YOUR POMERANIAN

A s any owner will tell you, once you have a Pomeranian, you'll never want another breed. These little guys have far more to their credit than just being a cute little Ewok of a dog. All of the genetics and all of the temperament choices Pomeranian breeders have made over the last thousand years were done with the purpose of creating a superb canine companion. Quite simply, Poms were bred to be the ultimate buddy.

PHYSICAL CHARACTERISTICS

The Pom is much more than just a pretty face, but as with any breed, the standard really does matter. A standard is a summary of the ideal attributes of a particular breed of dog—or in other words, the list of physical and mental characteristics that makes your Pom a Pom. The closer a dog adheres to those traits, the better his quality. Show breeders, in their efforts to improve the breed for future generations, are far more critical in looking over their stock than you will ever be in looking at your pet. But just because your dog isn't "show quality" doesn't mean that he isn't a wonderful companion or that he shouldn't look and act like a Pomeranian.

GENERAL APPEARANCE

The Pomeranian is a small dog of Nordic descent. His outercoat is long with harsh guard hairs set up over a thick undercoat. The square body, with a deep ruff around the neck and a heavily plumed, high-set tail lying flat on his back, gives him a somewhat round appearance. His tiny, erect ears are almost hidden in the fluff of his ruff hair. He is smart, alert, and buoyant. Characteristic of the breed is the "Pommie stare": head up, watching his owner intently to see what's going to happen next. Poms are quite sure that if they are not paying attention, they might miss something. This breed wants nothing more than to be a bright and cheerful companion.

Pom breeders have striven over the years to create the ultimate canine companion.

PUPPY POINTER

All Nordic breeds, from American Eskimos to Malamutes, from Shiba Inus to Akitas, resemble darling animated teddy bears as puppies. Pomeranians are no exception. Of course, all puppies are delightful, but the Nordic breeds have kicked up the puppy "aww" factor to the point where it can become an obsession. Pomeranians are a wonderful breed, and when thoroughly trained, they are the ultimate buddy, but they are not the right fit for every household. It is easy to fall in love with a puppy morsel that looks like a miniature Ewok, but you must evaluate a potential dog thoroughly before committing to him to ensure that you have the temperament and circumstances for this wonderful but sometimes demanding breed. Don't let the trimmings fool you into taking on a project you are not equipped to handle. That wouldn't be fair to anyone, and most importantly, it wouldn't be fair to your dog.

It can be interesting to navigate life with an independent and smarty-pants Pom. This breed can suffer from "small dog syndrome," a condition in which his human family treats him like precious nobility, turning him into a tyrant. A Pomeranian needs kind but thorough training. He can easily tap into his inner wolf; while he doesn't howl like one, a Pom may bark excessively, warning of incoming strangers, the passing of a bird overhead, or of grass moving in the breeze. An intelligent owner makes sure that her Pom is well socialized and respects household rules. In fact, Poms do best with owners who are as bright and confident as they are.

BODY TYPE: A BIG DOG IN A SMALL PACKAGE

Pomeranians are square and compact in size; they are short backed with a level topline and carry their head high. The standards of the American Kennel Club (AKC) and Fédération Cynologique Internationale (FCI, an international organization of kennel clubs) ask for a dog that is no greater than 7 pounds (3 kg). Most show dogs are at the top of their standard, and the majority of healthy Poms are at least 4 pounds (2 kg). Some pets can be 8 or even 10 pounds (3.5 or 4.5 kg). The 7 pounds (3 kg) asked for in the standard translates to a dog who is about 8 inches (20.5 cm) at the shoulder.

There is no discussion in any Pomeranian standard of "mini" or "teacup" Poms, and responsible breeders do not strive for a tiny-sized (under 3-pound [1.5-kg])

CHARACTERISTICS OF YOUR POMERANIAN

As with any dog, Pomeranians benefit from kind and positive training.

dog. While the Pomeranian is indeed one of the smallest dog breeds, it is very important to note that tiny dogs are often less healthy and shorter lived than their sturdier counterparts. Smaller may be a curiosity, but it is not better.

THE POM'S HEAD (...AND SHOULDERS, KNEES, AND TOES)

A Pom's cute head is a primary source of that "aw" factor. His muzzle is quite small in relation to his slightly rounded back skull. When looked at from above, it should form a distinct wedge shape. He has a pronounced stop (the point in front of the headpiece where the muzzle and skull join), and his ears are small, V-shaped, carried erect, and mounted high. He has medium-sized, almond-shaped eyes; they are dark chocolate, liquid, and full of intelligence. The eye rims are black except when he is chocolate colored, "beaver" (light brown), or blue, in which cases the eye rims are the same shade as the body coat.

Poms were carefully bred smaller from their bigger spitz cousins over the course of several hundred years. Even though their legs are shorter than those of their relatives, they should be straight, moderately angulated, and capable of strong and confident movement. His feet should be small and cat-like.

COAT: THE POM'S CROWNING GLORY

The Pomeranian has a double coat that stands out in a constant state of surprise—the long, harsh guard hairs stick out amidst a dense, short undercoat. With a ruff so big he can lay his head back against it, a deep, outstanding body coat, and a high-set, profusely feathered tail that lays flat against his body, an adult Pom in full coat can look as round as a dandelion seed. His legs are free of long hair and are covered with a dense mantle of short fur. Males have a more profuse coat than females do.

Most Poms that are not shown carry less coat and better resemble their spitz cousins, with a flatter neck ruff and shorter body coat.

Fur, Fur, and More Fur

All animals with hair shed to some degree and have dander (which is the real culprit in canine allergies). Some breeds, like the Maltese, have very little undercoat and so don't shed much. Other breeds, like the Pomeranian, have small clouds of fur following them. They shed constantly, with heavier sheds occurring twice a year, and are generally not appropriate for people with dog allergies.

To determine if your Pom puppy is going to be okay with your allergic family member, bring her along to see the puppies. Have her play with some adult dogs too. If the family member doesn't start sneezing at the breeder's house, she will probably be okay with the new puppy in your home.

A Coat of Many Colors

If a Pomeranian's fur is his crowning glory, then he is destined to shine in a coat of many colors. Poms come in more color variations than almost any other breed. Per the standard, all colors and patterns are allowed, although some are more popular than others. Colors include:

- **White:** Queen Charlotte's Poms were white. But as is often the case with genetics, the color of the dog was connected to his larger size, as well as a longer muzzle and larger ears. Eventually, breeders managed to bring the size down. Truly white Poms are highly sought after but

Dog Tale

The smallest Pomeranian on record was Tinkerbell, who at 14 weeks old was just less than 2 inches (5 cm) tall, the size of a medium espresso cup. Did she grow any bigger? There's no record of this. Gwenda Davidson from Cumbria, United Kingdom, was Tink's breeder.

remain hard to find.

- **Cream:** Cream is a variation of white—a very light liver or yellow. It occurred as a genetic "sport," or surprise, from black, white, shaded sables, or orange breedings. It is one color throughout with no white breechings or under-parts. Some people think that cream is a diluted orange, but it is its own unique color.
- **Black:** This color was extremely popular in the early 1900s, but when shaded sables came into existence, many black females were taken to other colors to produce this new, popular variation. Several current breeders are working hard to revitalize the true black, with no rust, white, or brown hairs.
- **Brown:** This covers all shades from brown-black umber through a medium brown milk chocolate to a beige beaver, which is rare. The umber is a rich and dark baker's chocolate, with no shade variations. Brown fades in sunlight and may carry a rusty tinge. The dog's eye rims, lips, and footpads are also brown and can be so dark as to appear black.
- **Blue:** This is another rare color that used to be popular. The color is extremely difficult to produce because it only can breed "true" (that is, by a blue to a blue). Puppies are born slate or black before developing a silvery gray undercoat with a darker blue topcoat, with a dark blue nose, eye rims, lips, and footpads.
- **Orange:** One of the most popular colors, orange is a bright, clear shade that varies from light to dark. Occasionally there are light shadings on the breeches or bibs. (Dark shadings would make the dog an orange sable.) A blonde is not really a cream but a very light orange with or without lighter and possibly white shadings.
- **Red:** This is not a dark orange but a deep, clear red.
- **Shaded Sables:** This coat color is shaded uniformly throughout with three or more colors. Sables generally have the best coat textures of any of the Pomeranian colors. An orange sable has a

Most Poms who are not going into the show ring resemble their spitz cousins, with a flatter neck ruff and shorter body coat.

light orange undercoat with deeper orange guard hairs ending in black tips. In red sables, the base colors are red tipped with black; creams are the same but exhibit a cream base. A wolf sable has a pewter undercoat with steel gray guard hairs ending in black tips. In a reverse sable, the undercoat and guard hair colors are reversed.

- **Parti-Color:** This is defined as a dog with more than one coat color on a white base. The colors should be evenly distributed, and ticking is discouraged. Preferred is a white blaze on the head. Partis occurred as a sport when breeding between whites, blacks, blues, and shaded sables. This is one of the original Pom color combinations, but in the past, partis have often also been oversized. Parti-color has become less common as breeders have attempted to maintain the pattern on a correctly sized dog. Variations of the parti-color are: extreme piebald (white with patches of color on the head and the base of the tail); piebald (white with patches of color on the head, body, and base of tail); and Irish (color on the head and body with white legs, chest, and collar).
- **Black-and-Tan:** These are black Poms with well-defined tan or rust patterns over the eyes, on both sides of the muzzle, on the throat, forechest, and legs, and below the tail. Because this color's base is black, not white as in the parti-color, the eye rims, lips, and footpads must be black.

LIVING WITH A POMERANIAN

Just like some people are social butterflies and some are wallflowers, some Poms may be a bit shy and some can be in-your-face confident. But like all purebred dogs, they share a certain range of temperament. For example, most Poms want to hang out with their owners. The joke around the Internet goes "How many Pomeranians does it take to switch a lightbulb? Just one, as long as you change it with him!"

A HEROIC BUDDY

In 1880, eight years before Queen Victoria met her Marco, a Pom named Bobby was just doing his job. Smuggled into the Royal Berkshire Regiment during the Anglo-Afghan War by soldiers far from home, Bobby traveled under his friends' shirts or perched jauntily atop backpacks during the long trek. This courageous and confident Pom knew that his job was simple: He had to keep his mates optimistic and happy. But during the chaos of the Battle of Maiwand, the British Army suffered one of its few Asian defeats. In the bedlam, Bobby was lost. His soldier friends were devastated. How could such a little mite survive such large havoc?

Bobby might have been small, but he was exceedingly tough. (It's not for nothing that the breed was developed by Vikings.) He survived with just a long scratch

Dog Tale

Carol Kingsley writes, "For about a year my Pom Tito and I lived on a horse farm. The place had a wonderful barn and stables, as well as a family of rabbits that lived under the tack room floor. They had burrowed under the barn with several entrances and exits. Tito, ferocious and fearless even though he only weighs 7 pounds (3 kg), discovered that giving chase to the rabbits was his favorite sport. Then one day he found the rabbit warren and realized he could go down the hole just like they did! But then he found that once he was in the ground, he couldn't turn around and get out.

"One day I noticed that Tito was missing. I called and called for him. Finally, I heard a muffled bark coming from under the tack room floor. I got a helper and we removed the floor boards. There he was, stuck curled up in the bottom of the rabbit warren. After a good bath, Tito decided that following the rabbits was still great sport—as long as he didn't have to go down their hole!"

down his back and was reunited with his old regiment.

Queen Victoria visited India a year later to give good conduct medals to the brave soldiers. Bobby attended, wearing a velvet coat embroidered with pearls and complete with two good conduct stripes. If you didn't know him, you'd think that Buddy was some cosseted milady's toy, but the reality was that he'd earned his stripes by doing his job: being a brave and excellent human companion.

Poms love to stick their chests out and strut their stuff, to act out being big and rough just like the traders who originally bred them. You can never convince a Pom that he is small or weak; he just won't believe you!

POMS AND CHILDREN

Poms can get along with children, but they are so cute and small that young kids often think of them as stuffed animals and try to treat them that way. Also, a Pom who is used to being the king of his household will not easily tolerate their noise and roughhousing. This is why kids and your Pom need a thorough understanding of their roles.

Often young children don't know their own strength and can literally suffocate a Pom with hugs. Many responsible breeders will not sell a Pomeranian puppy to a family with children under the age of five. But adult Poms are often surprisingly tolerant and can sometimes do well with even small children, as long as their parents supervise rigorously and give the Pom a breather if he needs it.

Even when you train your own child thoroughly in how to deal with your sometimes squirmy little dog, how should you handle her friends? Any child guest in your house should only hold the dog on the floor. Have her sit down and then put your Pom in her lap. This way, if the guest is distracted or the dog suddenly decides to take off, he won't fall far. Don't force any interactions; if your Pom is not happy, respect his wishes and remove him from the situation.

POMS AND OTHER DOGS

The Pomeranian can usually tolerate other dogs, and some get along quite well—in their own fashion. Coming from rough and tough stock and hardwired to take care of their humans, they will tolerate other dogs on their turf as long as everyone knows who rules the roost. Poms can even tolerate members of their own sex, which is unusual for toy breeds. But still, the best mix is a female and male together; a male will generally defer to a female.

Some Poms can even get along with big dogs, but in this area more than any other, they need a loving owner who is also an excellent trainer and can head off incipient dangers at the pass. Your big-talking Pom must never be allowed to tease

Although Poms can get along quite well with other dogs, they fare best with similar-sized canines.

his big cousin to the point of retaliation. This is why some breeders will not sell a Pom to a family with another dog over 50 pounds (22.5 kg).

ENVIRONMENT

Poms make wonderful suburban dogs because they do very well in apartments and require less exercise than many other breeds. They can be a city dweller's delight, a true come-along dog able to hang out wherever their owner has a mind to go. In the minus column, they are somewhat noisier than many other toy breeds, so you need tolerant neighbors. Poms can also make great country dogs as long as you aren't looking for a jogging partner.

EXERCISE

Poms are very active small dogs. They thoroughly enjoy a daily walk but are also small enough to get their exercise from a vigorous ball game or tug-of-war in the backyard. Poms basically just want to be with their owners. A leisurely stroll? Sure. Race around the backyard, chasing a ball? Absolutely. The Pom is a great breed for the country or the city; he can adjust his exercise requirements to fit his owner's lifestyle.

TRAINABILITY

For a breed made up of independent thinkers and original characters, the Pomeranian is remarkably trainable. They can also solve problems their owners did not foresee. (And sometimes even solve a problem that their owner never had!) Poms need to be trained with a light touch and lots of variety to prevent them from becoming bored. These little dogs have quick reaction times, possess a good sense of humor, and above all enjoy taking care of their owners. Many have even achieved advanced obedience degrees! Their ability to watch their owners with the famous "Pommie stare" allows them to keep up and follow quickly each command—if they feel like it, of course.

Is the Pomeranian actually any harder to housetrain than a bigger dog? Anecdotally, all small dogs are harder to housetrain than their bigger cousins; however, no one has done a real study on this. When a Lab puppy makes a mistake, the sheer size of the "oops" galvanizes everyone to do something about it. But when a Pom puppy makes a "cute little mistake," many owners think it's no big deal. Then this leniency becomes a habit, which becomes hard to eliminate. Your best bet is to adhere to a housetraining schedule right from the beginning.

WATCHDOG ABILITY

Poms make good watchdogs. They can be quite suspicious of strangers and will enthusiastically bark to alert to perceived trouble, be it a stranger or the squirrel two houses down. They are courageous and protective of their homes.

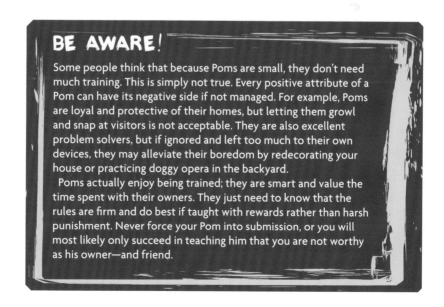

BE AWARE!

Some people think that because Poms are small, they don't need much training. This is simply not true. Every positive attribute of a Pom can have its negative side if not managed. For example, Poms are loyal and protective of their homes, but letting them growl and snap at visitors is not acceptable. They are also excellent problem solvers, but if ignored and left too much to their own devices, they may alleviate their boredom by redecorating your house or practicing doggy opera in the backyard.

Poms actually enjoy being trained; they are smart and value the time spent with their owners. They just need to know that the rules are firm and do best if taught with rewards rather than harsh punishment. Never force your Pom into submission, or you will most likely only succeed in teaching him that you are not worthy as his owner—and friend.

SUPPLIES FOR YOUR POMERANIAN

Ever since the smallest-sized spitz gained the Pomeranian moniker, Poms have been dogs of royalty. Far from home, English Queen Charlotte had a pair as a cure for homesickness. Later, granddaughter Queen Victoria fell in love with her Marco, and the breed was never the same again.

So it's logical that your Pom needs to always have the best of the best, right? You might be surprised. The fact is, an effective accessory for your Pom doesn't always have to be the most exclusive. For example, unless you plan to bring your Pom along to a movie premiere or two, bejeweled collars will not only break his coat but may give him deep scratches as well. No movie premieres in your near future? Skip the jewels.

The right stuff sometimes needs to be the finest quality—and other times simplest really is best.

BEDS

Poms can resemble a tawny dandelion puff, but underneath all that hair remains a real canine. Like other breeds, they fetch, carry, and move things around (including bedding) with their mouths, so choose a quality one that's thoroughly washable.

Dog beds don't last forever. If your Pom gets a hole in it, either sew the hole up promptly or throw it away. Dogs can get sick from eating stuffing or can get a limb caught in loose string or a hole.

Your Pom's bed should be both comfortable and washable.

Pomeranians have been called the ultimate companion dog; they definitely want to be with their human as much as they can possibly can. If you buy your Pom one lovely bed, he will happily use it—as long as you stay with him in that room. If you move, he will too. Your Pom just wants to hang with you, so keep in mind that he'll probably need a bed in every room of your house!

DONUT BEDS

A favorite Pom bed is the simple but highly practical "donut." It's shaped in a circle with a hole in the middle; the sides keep out drafts, and there is a usually a removable cushion in the "hole." Everything can be washed.

SATIN CUSHIONS

If you want to grow out your Pom's coat so that it's bushy and full, satin cushions can be helpful. They don't catch or break the coat as much as cotton or other fiber mixes do. Satin cushions can be difficult to find, but if you're handy with a sewing machine, you can easily make them yourself.

PVC BEDS

PVC beds comprise a simple stretch of fabric over plastic pipes, with four legs. Although they look more like a bench than a bed, Poms in hot climates love them because the elevated design allows nicely for cooling air circulation.

YOUR BED

Your Pom will likely jump at the chance to sleep with you, but beware of a bed that is too high for him. The rule of thumb is that if he can't climb onto it by himself, he won't be able to jump off of it safely by himself. You can purchase carpeted stairs that will help him climb up and down. However, even the mellowest Pom may try a flying leap to disaster if he thinks he will be left behind. If you have concerns about your Pom jumping off your bed, pick him up when you leave the room.

Your Pom's collar must be loose enough to slide easily onto his neck but not so loose that he can wiggle out of it.

COLLAR

All collars can break coat, and ideally nothing must get in the way of that big ruff. But in day-to-day life with doors that get left open and gates that don't get latched, your Pom needs a collar to keep him safe.

HOW TO CHOOSE THE RIGHT SIZE

You may need anywhere from an 8- to 14-inch (20.5- to 35.5-cm) collar for a Pomeranian depending on his size, the collar manufacturer, and the type of collar. If you buy a collar online, loop a string around his neck and measure the length with a ruler to arrive at the right size

The collar needs to be loose enough to slide easily onto your dog's neck but not so loose that he could wiggle out in a panic—rule of thumb is that you should be able to fit two fingers between the collar and your Pom's neck. If you can pull the collar over his head, it is too big.

COLLAR TYPES

There are a few different types of collars that are right for your Pom.

Rolled Leather

A rolled leather collar breaks coat the least. This collar is cylindrical with one seam rather than the usual two edges. These sturdy collars are a bit more expensive than others but are long lasting.

Nylon

Nylon collars are soft and comfortable. If your Pom has a short coat, this is a good, inexpensive choice. If you are trying to keep your dog in full coat, a nylon collar may break it.

High-End

As mentioned earlier, gemstone collars are not appropriate for your Pom. At best they will cut his coat and at worst they will cut his skin.

Harnesses

What about harnesses? Poms want to hang with you, but they also want to be in charge. Harnesses are often recommended for them by trainers who don't know better. A harness tends to teach a dog to pull. Sled dogs know this—they maximize their pulling abilities by pushing all their power against a central chest strap. Yes, your Pom may resemble a miniature sled dog, but do you really want him to pull like one? Harnesses have their place with Poms who have neck or trachea issues, but in general, a dog who hauls on the leash needs to learn his manners.

Some collars attach to a dog's muzzle, much like a horse's bridle. The theory is that if you can turn the dog's head, you can stop him from pulling. Such collars can be problematic for Pomeranians as their muzzles are so small, the device can fall off.

CRATE

Dogs are hardwired to be den animals, so they feel safest in small enclosed spaces. Don't think of a crate as a cage—think of it as a bedroom. And just like

Dogs are den animals, so most consider a crate to be a safe haven.

you sometimes want to have alone time with the door closed, most trained dogs consider their crates a safe haven and refuge. A crate-trained dog can be safe and secure in all circumstances, ranging from a short car trip to an overnight stay at Aunt Mildred's. They are an integral piece of equipment for your Pom's well-being.

HOW TO CHOOSE THE PROPER SIZE

A crate is the correct size when it allows your dog to stand up and turn around comfortably—and no more. A crate can definitely be too big; if your Pom can walk several steps, he may decide that it's convenient to sleep in one corner and go potty in the other. Once "trained" by you to do this, it's very hard to break the habit.

CRATE TYPES

There are a few different types of crates.

Wire

These crates can be found anywhere from a discount retailer to a high-end boutique. They can be fine as your dog's house crate because they let lots of air circulate but are not good for travel of any sort. In an accident, the wires could come loose during impact and injure your Pom.

A good carry bag with sturdy handles is perfect for taking your Pom along with you when traveling!

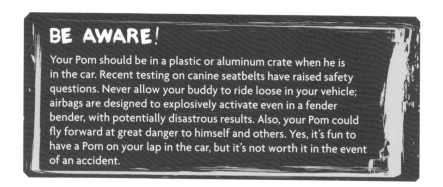

Plastic, Metal, or Wooden

Plastic or aluminum metal crates are excellent for travel; they are lightweight and extremely sturdy. Plastic crates are considerably cheaper. Decorative wooden crates are much heavier but look nice because they can be crafted to resemble high-end furniture. (They also carry a high-end price tag!)

Soft-Sided

Soft-sided crates are made of nylon and PVC pipes. They shouldn't be used in a car because they will collapse in any kind of crash. These lightweight crates make a small package in your suitcase and can easily be put up at your destination, but not all Poms do well in them. They are so light that some determined dogs can move them across a room by repeatedly banging against the sides.

Carry Bags

Poms are definitely take-along dogs. Their strong desire to go everywhere with their owners, along with their small size, makes them the ideal companion. But even the smallest dogs sometimes needs containment; they require a bag of the correct size with sturdy handles. Most large purses are plenty big enough, and a small towel placed at the bottom will make it a bit more comfortable.

Airline Bags

Even your small buddy can get surprising heavy when you are running to your plane, so an ideal airline bag has wheels and a telescoping handle to pull behind you. The bag needs to be tall enough so that your Pom can sit up fully when upright and long enough so that when slid under the seat in front of you, he can stretch out. It also needs to have plenty of mesh, as the space under the seat in front of you can get pretty hot. An ideal bag has a wide base and a narrow top.

DOGGY GATES

A good house containment system, especially when your Pom is young, will keep him safe and can make all the difference to your blood pressure. Temporary gates allow you to set up the living space for your Pom as needed. They secure to a doorway with pressure clamps. If you need a more permanent solution, consider custom-made iron gates, which are beautiful and surprisingly affordable.

EXERCISE PEN (EX-PEN)

Ex-pens are containment systems comprising nylon or wire and have no floor. If you need to leave your young Pom at home for more than several hours, these pens make a great enclosure.

FOOD AND WATER BOWLS

You can choose from among a few types of food and water bowls.

STAINLESS STEEL

Stainless steel dishes are easy to clean and won't break, but some are also somewhat lightweight. A determined Pomeranian can entertain himself for several hours by playing soccer with his bowl, spilling his water or food in a nice even layer all over the floor. An alternative is a weighted bowl or one that fits into a ring in your Pom's crate, which will curtail his soccer career.

CERAMIC

These are heavier and so a good choice if you have a Pom practicing for FC Madrid, but they're also breakable. Care must be also taken that the glaze is food grade because some lovely ceramics use glazes that contain lead, which is poisonous to your Pom.

PLASTIC

Plastic dishes are not recommended; they are too light and can easily develop hard-to-clean scratches that harbor bacteria.

BE AWARE!

Nordic breeds are adaptable to many climates, but if you want your Pomeranian to maintain the characteristic full, off-standing coat you see at dog shows, a cool environment is best. If you live in a warmer area, keep him cool or he will "blow," or lose, his full undercoat, causing the rest of his hair to lie flat.

GROOMING SUPPLIES

Even if you don't plan to do all of your Pomeranian's grooming yourself, you should have the following:

- **4- or 5-inch (10- or 12-cm) scissors.** Blunt-end scissors can give a novice groomer confidence that she won't stab her dog. (You won't stab your dog, but really only experience will teach you this.)
- **4- or 5-inch (10- or 12-cm) thinning shears.** Select shears containing teeth on one side only—these will remove less coat than double-sided thinning shears.
- **Quality electric clippers.** Corded clippers last forever, but you'll feel a bit like a pretzel getting into the small in-between bits on your dog. Cordless clippers are much more convenient, but even the highest-priced rechargeable battery will eventually wear out, and most clippers don't have a replaceable battery—you have to buy a whole new machine. No matter which type you choose, make sure that the clippers are made for dogs and not people. Human clippers have a high-pitched whine that we can't hear—but your Pom can.
- **Greyhound-style metal comb.** This comb checks for coat tangles. Keep in mind that inexpensive combs have very small bumps or burrs on the metal that can tear up your Pom's coat, so spend a little more money to get a quality comb.

A good pair of blunt-edged scissors and greyhound-style metal comb will help you start your grooming experience.

- **Undercoat rake.** Undercoat rakes are specifically made for dogs with a thick undercoat, like your Pom. The thin tines allow you to really get into your dog's hair and pull out any loose undercoat without dislodging the longer guard hairs.
- **Slicker brush.** Slicker brushes can get into thick coats easier than a regular brush. Select a small one with extra-thin tines so that you can get into tight spaces.
- **Soft pin brushes.** Use this type of brush to smooth the coat; it doesn't detangle.
- **Grooming arm.** Pomeranians can be wriggly, and a grooming arm holds at least their head in place.

You simply clamp the arm on the edge of a table to secure your dog. They can be found on pet-supply websites.

- **Grooming table.** A grooming table is certainly nice but may not be necessary. You just need some sort of nonslip surface, preferably with a lip, where you can clamp a grooming arm. A sturdy nonslip bathmat paced on a high counter (so that you don't have to bend) will work well.
- **Shampoo/conditioner and leave-in conditioner.** You want the hair products especially made for your Pom's thick Nordic coat.
- **Hairspray/mousse/gel.** If you are really aiming for the dandelion look, follow the show handler trick. When still damp, massage some gel or hairspray at the base of your Pom's coat. Blow out as usual and his naturally great puffball look will last and last.
- **Nail clippers.** Get the kind for the biggest breeds. They will clip your little dog's toenails that much easier.
- **Toothbrush and toothpaste.** Pomeranians have miniaturized mouths (as do most small dogs), so their teeth don't have a lot of room, crowding them and making them susceptible to decay and tooth loss. A weekly tooth brushing is a must to keep your Pom's gums and teeth strong and healthy.

IDENTIFICATION

Who owns your dog? Well, you do, of course. But can you prove this? And why would you want to? If your dog ever gets loose, you need to be able to prove that your Pom is your Pom. With conclusive identification, you can verify ownership.

MICROCHIPS

Microchips have become very popular over the last decade. This rice-sized pellet of glass contains a unique identifying number and is embedded under the skin at your Pom's shoulder with a syringe. Collars can come off and tags can be removed, but microchips provide permanent proof that your Pom really is yours.

TAGS

Tags are useful in addition to a microchip, but rather than having a jangling array, all you need are the following:

- **Rabies tag:** If lost, an animal control officer can find you via your Pom's tag records. Also, if he is found and doesn't carry his rabies tag, he could be quarantined to ensure that he doesn't have rabies.
- **Microchip tag:** This tag proves to a casual person that your Pom is not a stray but a beloved member of someone's family. And of course, he can be identified and returned to you.
- **ID tag:** If your Pom gets loose, he will most likely get picked up by your neighbor or someone on your street. With an ID tag, your neighbor can call you right away.

LEASHES

Poms need two basic types of leashes.

WALKING LEASHES

Walking leashes are about 4 to 6 feet (1 to 2 m) long and are perfect for a brisk stroll. You don't want a retractable leash for walks because you need to keep your Pom close by. Good walking leashes can be made out of leather or nylon—they can be country-club fine, downtown wild, or strictly utilitarian. Just make sure that the leash you choose has a small, sturdy clasp.

RETRACTABLE LEASHES

Retractable leashes are perfect for a romp. In a calmer day and age, you could clip your dog to a leash to walk along the street, then let him loose to play at the park. But no longer. A loose Pom, even when well trained, is not a good idea. However, a retractable leash offers a good compromise. It has a plastic handle with a spring-loaded cord connected to a regular leash. Your Pom can run out to the end of the leash (as much as 15 feet [4.5 m]), then roar back in to make sure

A good walking leash is perfect for a brisk stroll and for keeping your Pom close.

that you are okay. The spring winds up the long leash out of the way as he slides in for a landing.

ODOR-REMOVING CLEANSER

Poms will occasionally do doggy things like take apart the garbage or leave muddy footprints all over the kitchen floor. Even households with "royal" dogs can benefit from canine-strength odor-removing cleansers. The best ones have a citrus base; they come highly concentrated (you generally put two fingers in the bottom of a spray bottle and fill it up with water), and a gallon (4 l) lasts forever.

TOYS

Poms love their toys. They entertain themselves with them for hours and will use them to entertain you for hours as well.

STUFFED TOYS

If your Pom was stranded on a desert island, which one toy would he take? Probably a stuffed one! They chew on them, carry them as security blankets, or play tug-of-war with them. Just make sure that your Pom's are made for dogs, not people. Dogs use their teeth to handle things, so even your little Pom will be hard on Teddy. His toys' stuffing also needs to be canine approved—as in not poisonous. Some toys made for humans use stuffing that can be dangerous if ingested.

SQUEAKY TOYS

Dogs, as hardwired predators, love things that squeak. The noise they make is a fun surprise, and Poms have a great time making the toy do it again and again. If your Pom enjoys determinedly taking apart a toy to get at the squeaker, though, be careful. This hard plastic mechanism can lodge in his gut and necessitate an expensive trip to the emergency room. If your Pom gets that certain glint in his eye when presented with a squeaky toy, you might want to consider alternative entertainment.

HARD RUBBER TOYS

Hard rubber toys are essentially indestructible but may have a strong smell when first purchased. A couple of trips through the washing machine can help. These toys are perfect treat delivery devices and can keep your Pom intrigued for hours as he tries to get the last bit of kibble or last lick of peanut butter out of the toy's middle.

Dog Tale

Elise Morrison writes the following: "Rocky got his stuffed iguana 'Iggy' soon after he came to live with us. It was his 'greeting' toy. When one of his special people arrived, he had to have Iggy in his mouth to say hello. Over time Iggy got pretty beat up, so one day I gave the toy to my mother-in-law to repair and put out a stuffed green frog of about the same size. That evening I came home late. Rocky wouldn't greet me. He ignored the frog and circled through the house searching disconsolately for his special toy. Despite the late hour I had to drive over to my mother-in-law's to get Iggy. I eventually ended up repairing the iguana myself while Rocky slept."

CHAPTER 4

FEEDING YOUR
POMERANIAN

Your Pomeranian's health and happiness are inseparable from a diet that fulfills his nutritional needs. Basically, your Pom is what he eats. A good diet supplies him with energy, nutrition, and enough surface abrasion to reduce tartar. Most importantly, your Pom needs a diet that he likes and that he is willing to eat. The most balanced diet in the world will be useless if your Pom turns his nose up at it.

NUTRITION BASICS

Your Pom requires more than just calories to thrive. He needs the correct balance of carbohydrates, fats, and proteins, as well as the right mix of vitamins and minerals. Dogs don't crave the variety of diet that most humans do; just like the child who happily eats peanut butter and jelly sandwiches for lunch year after year, your Pom will be perfectly happy with a diet of the same old same old, as long as it tastes good and meets all his nutritional needs.

CARBOHYDRATES

Carbohydrates are organic compounds made up of a combination of sugars, starch, and cellulose and can be broken down to release energy. Immediate energy comes from carbs, and the carbohydrate fiber or cellulose becomes

Feeding your Pomeranian a nutritionally balanced diet that appeals to his appetite will help him live a long, healthy life.

roughage that keeps you Pom's digestive system moving along smoothly. Complex carbohydrates such as whole grains are especially important because they break down into sugar slower than simple carbs do, providing a more sustained energy source. Carbohydrates from rice are best utilized; descending from rice are potato, corn, wheat, oats, and beans, in that order. Carbs should compose about 50 percent of your Pom's diet.

FATS

Fats are a greasy mixture of lipids. They not only provide a quick surge of energy but are also vital for skin and hair health, especially the omega-3 and omega-6 fatty acids. The correct balance of fats keeps skin supple and healthy and the hair shafts strong and smooth. Without sufficient fat, your Pom's coat will become dull and brittle. What is enough fat? About 18 percent of his total nourishment is ideal. Omega-3s come from fish and flaxseed oil; omega-6s come from seed and nut oils.

PROTEINS

Proteins comprise amino acids and are the body's primary building block, creating sturdy bones and strong muscles. They also provide long-lasting energy. Your Pom needs the right kind of protein to grow and maintain his glorious outsides—and insides too. His food should be 25 to 35 percent protein. Chicken, beef, lamb, and salmon provide excellent sources of protein.

VITAMINS

Vitamins are organic substances, needed in the correct amount and in the correct balance to maintain and regulate body functions. Poms in particular require plenty of B-complex with an emphasis on biotin, also known as the skin vitamin, to maintain their thick dandelion coat. B-complex comes from meat products such as liver, turkey, and tuna, as well as potatoes, bananas, lentils, beans, brewer's yeast, and molasses. Other vitamins are essential as well, such as glucosamine, which promotes joint health. Certain vitamins, such as vitamin E and B complex, need to be in correct ratio to each other to work well. Vitamin E is an antioxidant, while vitamin B balances cholesterol and has been known to aid brain function. Because both basically help keep cells "clean," they work well together.

Correctly maintained, a good vitamin mix minimizes future health problems.

MINERALS

Minerals are inorganic substances, and just like vitamins, the correct balance is essential to your Pom's good health. He needs both calcium and phosphorus, as well as other trace minerals such as iron, copper, zinc, and manganese, for optimum metabolism and to help keep his coat healthy.

WATER
Your Pom must have easy access to cool, clean water to maintain good health. Water hydrates his cells and keeps nutrients, vitamins, and minerals flowing in and the waste flowing out.

DOG FOOD LABELS
Dog food labels contain two main parts: the guaranteed analysis and the ingredient list.

GUARANTEED ANALYSIS
The guaranteed analysis provides a breakdown of the food, listing which substances in the brand are present, in what percentage. Use caution when comparing two different foods to make sure that moisture is taken into account, as this will otherwise skew the numbers; totals are measured by the complete food including moisture, but different brands have varying amounts of liquid.

Make sure that your Pomeranian always has access to plenty of cool, clean water.

INGREDIENT LIST

The ingredients are listed on the package in order of weight, with the heaviest first. Does that mean that the first ingredient, usually a protein, is the largest component of the food? Well, sometimes—and sometimes not. A favorite tactic of many major food manufacturers is to divide substances considered "less desirable" into several subcategories. This makes the protein component by default suddenly "become" the major ingredient. If you see corn, corn gluten meal, dried corn juice, and so forth all listed separately on the ingredients list, combine them to get a better idea of what is really the prevailing ingredient in your Pom's food.

There can be some odd-sounding ingredients listed in almost all dog food labels. This is what they really are:

- **Meat by-products** are animal parts but not meat. They include organs, blood, bone, and some fatty tissue. They do not include hair, horns, teeth, or hooves.
- **Poultry by-products** are parts of the chicken such as heads, feet, and organs. They do not contain feathers.
- **Brewer's rice** are fragmented rice kernels separated from milled rice. Brewer's rice, which contains the whole kernel, is healthier than milled or "white" rice.
- **Beet pulp** is the dried residue of sugar beets added for fiber and to add sweetness. Dogs apparently like sweet stuff just as much as we humans do!
- **Corn gluten meal** is the dried residue left after the removal of bran, germ, and starch.
- **Animal digest** is a powdered broth (think bouillon cubes) of any animal matter, excluding hooves and feathers.

Before you decide that all the above sounds barbaric and that the only good dog food should either be made by you or contain super-expensive human-grade

Should Pom puppies be fed differently than adults? Absolutely. Because any weaned puppy less than 2 pounds (1 kg) can be susceptible to hypoglycemia, Pom puppies must be fed at least four small meals a day, supplemented with two small knobs of high-calorie paste twice a day. He should also eat a special small-dog puppy formula until he is at least six months old. Leave out a bowl of dry kibble for him at all times (as long as he doesn't inhale his food), but also give him several set meals as well. Pick up these meals after about an hour.

Pomeranians like to nibble and so should have dry food available in case they get hungry.

ingredients, realize that all of these ingredients, when produced correctly, provide wholesome nutrition. Your Pom will happily devour them, lick his chops, and ask for more.

HOW TO FEED YOUR POM

If your Pom turns his nose up at his food, he certainly won't get its nutritional benefits. Remember the old wives' tale that healthy food had to taste bad? How about those spoonfuls of cod liver oil you gulped down as a child? Fortunately, healthy food can also be yummy. And if it tastes good, your Pom will be willing to eat it.

Some Poms like a bit of canned food mixed into their kibble with warm water, while some fare better with dry food. Your Pom will quickly let you know his ideal feeding regimen.

CALORIE REQUIREMENTS

Your Pomeranian is an active little guy who needs far more calories per pound (kg) than his bigger canine cousins. A good benchmark for Pom nutrition is to ensure that he receive about 300 calories per cup of food. Refer to the following

POMERANIAN

chart to determine how much food your Pom requires per day, depending on how much he weighs:

WEIGHT (POUNDS)	WEIGHT MAINTENANCE (CUPS)
1	1/4
3	1/4
5	1/3
8	1/2
10	2/3
12	2/3
15	3/4

Keep in mind that these numbers are averages and will fluctuate depending on your adult Pom's activity level.

FREE-FEEDING VERSUS SCHEDULED FEEDING

Most Poms won't scarf down their food all at once—they like to nibble and so should have dry food available in case they get hungry. But they also require at least two scheduled meals a day. Many Poms prefer moistened meals of some sort, which you should pick up after a half hour. Of course, if your dog is one of those rare Poms who feels that mealtime is an eating contest and that he who finishes first wins, he should have three small set meals a day. Don't worry about picking up the leftovers after 30 minutes—you won't have any.

COMMERCIAL FOODS

Are commercial dog foods right for your Pom? Maybe. After a massive recall of kibble coming from overseas a couple of years ago, dog food companies are more

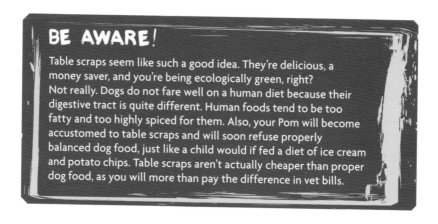

BE AWARE!

Table scraps seem like such a good idea. They're delicious, a money saver, and you're being ecologically green, right? Not really. Dogs do not fare well on a human diet because their digestive tract is quite different. Human foods tend to be too fatty and too highly spiced for them. Also, your Pom will become accustomed to table scraps and will soon refuse properly balanced dog food, just like a child would if fed a diet of ice cream and potato chips. Table scraps aren't actually cheaper than proper dog food, as you will more than pay the difference in vet bills.

vigilant than ever in making sure that their products are well crafted, balanced, nutritious, and wholesome. This is, after all, a good business model. If dogs eat the company's food and do well, their owners will be loyal to the brand. All quality commercial dog foods are certified by the Association of American Feed Control Officials (AAFCO); look for that designation when starting your search for the ideal food for your Pom.

As discussed earlier, Pomeranians require a specific balance of nutrition, so keep this in mind when researching foods. He also requires a small-sized kibble with the right amount of abrasion to control tartar.

Commercial foods come tailor-made for every life situation imaginable. There are puppy foods, senior foods, food for active canines, and diet foods. Some breeds are lucky enough to have foods made especially for them. Foods even exist to help manage a variety of medical conditions, usually available only from a vet. Just remember: The fanciest food imaginable will do your Pom no good if it doesn't appeal to his palate.

DRY FOOD

Commercial kibble is easy to use and ready to feed right out of the bag. It also often has built-in tartar-reducing abrasion. This convenient option also tends to be less expensive than home-cooked food.

To determine which dry food is right for your Pom, ask yourself these questions:
- **Does this food have the correct nutritional mix for Pomeranians?** Does it have meat as the first ingredient and approximately 30 percent proteins, 15 percent fats, and 50 percent carbohydrates?
- **Does this food make me consider taking out a second mortgage?** Quality kibble ranges widely in price. The most expensive variety is not necessarily the only one that will do the trick.
- **How active is my dog?** The higher protein and fat percentages might actually be detrimental for your Pom if he is more of a couch potato than backyard racing fiend.

You are going to have to try out several brands to see which your Pom likes best. Actually, it's probably better to buy your Pom's kibble in small quantities, as quality food usually has limited preservatives.

CANNED FOOD

Think that canned food is pure protein? Think again. It usually contains a similar formula to kibble but has a high percentage of water. Canned is best used as a sort of gravy over dry food; you should also add a couple of teaspoons of warm water if

Canned food is best used as a sort of gravy over dry food.

it's coming out of the fridge, as most dogs like their food cozily warmed. Canned food is not a good idea on its own for a Pom because it won't reduce tartar.

SEMI-MOIST FOOD

Semi-moist dog food has the consistency of fruit leather and is generally formed into mock hamburger-like patties or sausages. It won't turn into gravy, so it can't be used to moisten dry food. It also has a lot of sugar to prevent spoilage, so it's not good for your Pom's teeth.

NONCOMMERCIAL FOODS

Noncommercial foods are made by you, at home, using some sort of a formula. Because they aren't manufactured under rigorous factory standards, the nutritional mix may not be as precise as commercial foods. However, if you are willing to put in the time and do the research, noncommercial foods can be a viable alternative to commercial options.

HOME-COOKED DIET

Following the dog food scares in recent years, there are certainly some advantages to making your Pom's food yourself. One of the biggest benefits is that when you use quality, human-grade ingredients, you know exactly what he's eating.

Some good recipes for homemade dog food are available online. But even with the right formula, if you aren't precise in your measurements and rigorous in following directions, your

Dog Tale

Marsha Pugh writes: "I have cooked for my dogs for years. It isn't hard, but I rely on 'Monica Segal K9 Kitchen' as a guide to ensure that I am using the correct nutrients if I go totally home-cooked. Otherwise, I pour it over a little holistic kibble. I make up a two-week supply at one time in a pressure cooker, divide it into daily servings, and freeze it in microwave-safe containers. It's been my routine forever."

FEEDING YOUR POMERANIAN

Pom can end up with a food that isn't right for him. The right food with the correct mix of nutrients, along with the right amount of abrasion, can extend your Pom's life, but the wrong diet can shorten it. It's quite a commitment to make your Pom's food yourself, but some owners wouldn't do it any other way.

Vegetables are the healthiest treats. Chopped carrots, broccoli, and cauliflower have a nice satisfying crunch!

RAW DIET

Proponents of a raw diet (referred to as Bones and Raw Food [BARF]) believe that because dogs didn't eat cooked food when they were wolves, they shouldn't eat cooked food today. They feel that eating a mix of uncooked meat, ground raw bones, and vegetables is better for dogs. However, studies have not yet found this to be true, and no American, British, or Canadian veterinary associations have endorsed such diets. There is also concern that eating raw meat can lead to food poisoning, and the bone meal can stop up your Pom's short digestive tract.

TREATS

Commercial dog treats are great at advertising, but that's really all that can be said of most of them. Many dog treats are overly processed, overly sweet calorie bombs that your Pom either won't touch or will like so well that he'll turn down his regular chow. Much better are natural treats like real bones (raw, not cooked, which could splinter and cause digestive tract damage). Some commercial treats reduce tartar when chewed; these are okay on a limited basis.

Purchase your Pom's bones from a pet store; that way, you will know that they have been properly processed for dogs. Some bones have a neat hole in the middle that's perfect for inserting a mix of peanut butter and kibble for a long-lasting treat.

Of course, vegetables are the healthiest treats. Any veggie with a satisfying crunch will do; some good ones include carrots, broccoli, and cauliflower.

DIET ISSUES

Your Pomeranian is an energetic ball of fluff that requires a very specific nutritional mix to do his best. Fed correctly, he can remain a treasured companion for years to come; if not, he can suffer from food-related issues such as picky eating, obesity, and hypoglycemia.

PICKY EATING

Remember that day your Pom kept staring at your pocket until you pulled out the forgotten cookie wrapper? That was when you realized his nose was far more sensitive than a human's. Dogs can smell much better than we humans can, and Pomeranians are no exception. What you perhaps didn't know is that a dog's sense of taste is not as accurate as a human's (although the day you found your Pom happily rooting through the overturned garbage can might have been an indicator).

Dogs taste primarily through their sense of smell, but not all dog noses are created equal. German Shepherd Dogs, for example, have 200 million olfactory cells in their noses; Pomeranians have about 60 million. Because the Pom can't "taste" as well through his nose as his bigger cousins can, he needs a highly palatable food to be an eager trencherman. He will most likely refuse dog foods that more sensitive-nosed canines would eagerly inhale.

Dog Tale

Charley McDougall writes: "One day, my Sunny turned her nose up at her normal kibble, which was unusual for her. I didn't like the idea of her not eating, so I offered her some of my boneless chicken breast. She ate it with relish. But the next day, she didn't want her kibble again; all she seemed to want was that chicken breast. However, after a while she didn't want that either. So I moved onto turkey and then salmon and then—well, you get the idea. Finally, I didn't know what to feed her, so I called a friend who also has a Pomeranian. She was very polite, but I could hear the laughter in her voice.

"'Sunny's got you over a barrel!' she said. 'The solution is pretty easy. Feed her on a regular basis with her normal chow. She will turn her nose up at it. Remove the bowl after 30 minutes. After a day or so, she won't have the luxury of being picky anymore, and she'll start eating decent food again. My Pixie did this to me last year. After three days, she was back to eating normally.'

"It took Sunny four nerve-wracking days, but she finally realized that the gourmet food truck had permanently closed its doors. Lesson learned!"

As his sense of smell is less sensitive, he needs food with more punch to know that's it's the good stuff.

OBESITY

Most Poms are active little guys who don't become overweight easily. But older, sedentary dogs can occasionally pack on the pounds (kg), and for a small breed like the Pomeranian, it doesn't take much for him to become unhealthily obese.

If you need to put your dog on a diet, reduce his calorie intake by replacing some of the bulk of his food with an additive such as cooked green beans or plain air-popped popcorn.

Your mini butterball also needs more exercise. Whether it's a brisk walk or chasing a ball in the backyard, regular exercise will firm up your Pom, and when combined with a sensible diet, the weight will soon come off.

HYPOGLYCEMIA

Pomeranians—especially those under 2 pounds (1 kg)—are susceptible to hypoglycemia, a condition characterized by a sudden drop in glucose (sugar) in their system, resulting in loss of coordination, sleepiness, and lack of appetite. If untreated, hypoglycemia can lead to seizures, unconsciousness, and death. If your

If you find your Pom putting on weight, increase his exercise with a brisk walk or throw a ball for a good game of chase.

Pom is very small (under 3 pounds [1.5 kg]), he must be fed several small meals during the day rather than one or two big ones.

Pom puppies are especially susceptible to hypoglycemia because they don't have many fat deposits. The condition may also be related to immature liver cells. The connection between immature liver cells and hypoglycemia hasn't been absolutely established yet, but most vets will tell you that many super-small dogs or puppies also have liver disorders.

Small puppies (under 2 pounds) of any breed don't have enough fat deposits to keep up their energy without very frequent, small meals. Without this they can suddenly faint. After weaning, be sure to feed your under-2-pound (1-kg) puppy at least every four hours, and give him ¼ teaspoon of a high-calorie paste twice a day.

If you think that your Pom is experiencing a hypoglycemic episode, don't panic. You need a clear head to help your buddy right away. Feed him a high-glycemic food such as Karo syrup. If he can't swallow, rub some on his gums. Don't try to force food down his throat because he could choke. Wrap him up well to keep him warm, and call your vet or emergency clinic to tell them you are on the way. They will administer intravenous glucose if needed.

DENTAL HEALTH

Your Pom is about one quarter the size of the original spitzes that Queen Charlotte brought to England, so his teeth are crowded in a small jaw. Because the teeth are harder to clean, Poms are especially prone to dental problems, including gum disease. Brush your dog's teeth regularly and feed a tartar-preventive diet.

CHAPTER 5

GROOMING YOUR
POMERANIAN

There is nothing more striking than a Pomeranian in full coat, a miniature powder puff, his bushy coat fanning out all around him in arrested symmetry. The correct grooming is vital to creating this look, but it can be surprisingly easy if you know how to do it. A full show coat is truly stunning; fortunately, it only takes a short time to maintain a pet version of this coat.

WHY GROOMING IS IMPORTANT

Unless you plan to keep your Pom shaved to the skin, he needs to be groomed on a regular basis. This isn't just for cosmetic effect—a well-groomed dog is also healthier. Thick, dirty mats can infect the skin beneath, and regular brushing and bathing provide excellent opportunities to discover many incipient health problems, from ticks to skin tumors, before they have a chance to become major difficulties.

Grooming should also be a relaxing time, a special moment between you and your buddy. Just like humans might enjoy a bubble bath after a long day, a well-trained dog accepts and even enjoys his pampering.

Do you think that the only people who should touch your Pom with a brush are the professionals? Well, a Pomeranian is actually a pretty easy-care dog once you understand a couple of basics. Even if you decide to have a pro do any needed trimming, you can perform regular brushing and any needed bathing yourself.

GROOMING SUPPLIES

Your Pomeranian's thick double coat needs specialized brushes and combs intended to get down to his skin and loosen up incipient mats, to take out bits and pieces caught in his coat, and to loosen and remove his shedding undercoat before it covers your favorite carpet. He also requires additional grooming tools like nail clippers and dental cleaning supplies.

Here is a rundown of exactly what you'll need:

4" OR 5" SCISSORS

These can be purchased at a beauty supply store. Get scissors with blunt ends if you'd like; they will give you the secure feeling that you're not about to jab your dog.

4" OR 5" THINNING SHEARS

Thinning shears can be helpful to trim stray hairs on the ears or around the feet. They leave a cut that is a bit "ragged," with lots of different cut lengths, so that it looks more natural. The more teeth the scissors have, the less hair they take out with each cut, so in this case, more teeth is better.

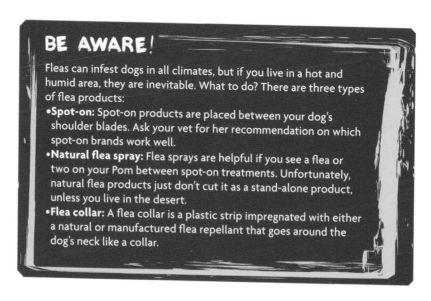

BE AWARE!

Fleas can infest dogs in all climates, but if you live in a hot and humid area, they are inevitable. What to do? There are three types of flea products:
- **Spot-on:** Spot-on products are placed between your dog's shoulder blades. Ask your vet for her recommendation on which spot-on brands work well.
- **Natural flea spray:** Flea sprays are helpful if you see a flea or two on your Pom between spot-on treatments. Unfortunately, natural flea products just don't cut it as a stand-alone product, unless you live in the desert.
- **Flea collar:** A flea collar is a plastic strip impregnated with either a natural or manufactured flea repellant that goes around the dog's neck like a collar.

BLOW-DRYER

The best blow-dryer for the Pom uses forced air that literally blows the water off his coat and quickly dries him down to his skin. Online pet stores sell forced air blow-dryers for fairly reasonable prices. Your own blow-dryer set to low heat will work, but the forced-air kind is best.

UNDERCOAT RAKE

The undercoat rake will remove loose undercoat and break up small tangles before they can turn into a solid mat of felt.

SLICKER BRUSH

This brush is good at getting to the bottom of your Pom's cloud of hair but won't take out as much undercoat as the rake. The fine wire won't break his hair.

SOFT PIN BRUSH

Soft pin brushes work well to smooth the coat, but they will not de-mat the undercoat, which can turn to a thick felt if unattended. Long-tined pin brushes work best for Poms.

GREYHOUND-STYLE METAL COMB

Good-quality metal combs are smooth and don't have microscopic burrs on their teeth that can break the coat. This is one area where you need to buy the best. The smaller-sized metal combs work well as face combs. Choose a metal comb that has widely spaced tines on one side and closely spaced tines on the other. You use the wider tines to tease out tangles; the finer ones will smooth out a fully brushed coat.

A blow-dryer that uses forced air is the best type to use for a Pomeranian with his thick undercoat because it will be able to dry him down to his skin.

HAIR CLIPPERS

Don't buy hair clippers from a beauty-supply store. Those intended for humans have a high-pitched whine that is unintelligible to us, but dogs can hear it; and in this case, they don't like what they hear. Corded clippers are longer lasting, but cordless ones are more convenient. They are very helpful in taking the hair off the inside of your Pom's ears and out from between the pads of his feet. If you plan to do a teddy bear clip yourself, you'll need clippers to create an even length of a velvety inch (2.5 cm) all over.

GROOMING ARM

Poms can be wriggly. A grooming arm, clamped to the side of a table, holds at least the head in place. You can purchase one on a pet-supply website.

GROOMING TABLE

Do you really need a grooming table? No, but a comfortable, stable table is a must, and you definitely need some sort of nonslip surface (at a comfortable level for you) where your dog feels secure. A nonslip bathmat placed on a counter works well for this.

NAIL CLIPPERS

Get the nail clippers made for the biggest breeds—they are more powerful even on small toenails. Scissors types are the best because it's easier to see the nail. Nail grinders are also available—they use a small revolving drum of sandpaper to grind down the nail, and dogs tolerate a grinder much better than nail clippers. However, while this tool can be extremely useful with a short-coated dog, a wiggly Pom's hair could easily become caught in the revolving shaft of the nail grinder's drum, causing the hair to be pulled out by the roots. Use a nail grinder with care!

SHAMPOO AND CONDITIONER

Your Pomeranian should only be bathed when necessary; bathing too often will soften his hair and deflate that great bushy Pommie look. He requires a shampoo and conditioner especially made for a Nordic double coat. And because a Pom always needs to be brushed when damp, a spray bottle filled with some sort of canine-only leave-in conditioner is a must. Children's detangler spray conditioners also work well.

DRY SHAMPOO/BABY POWDER

Sometimes your Pom will need to be freshened up or detangled when you don't want to bathe him. Baby powder or dry shampoo will help cleanse your Pom without adding water. Only use this if you have a forced air dryer, though, because that's the only way you'll be able to get the powder out of his coat.

COAT AND SKIN CARE

Pomeranians, like most Nordic breeds, are double coated. They have a thick undercoat and long guard hairs that separate the wool and create air pockets next to the skin. This is why your buddy can not only withstand cold temperatures but also stays surprisingly cool in hot weather. However, the undercoat wool must be kept unmatted so that the guard hairs can do their job.

Coat care is much more than making your Pom pretty—it also keeps him healthy. If you allow him to remain matted, you'll soon have a dog covered with sores, as the thick woolly felt covering his skin won't allow it to breathe.

It's best to brush your Pom when he is damp, after a bath or after lightly spritzing him with a leave-in conditioner.

Professional groomers only have a certain amount of time to spend on each dog, but that's not the case for you! If one procedure sends your Pom over the edge, take your time and break it down into smaller bits. This will not only save his (and your) sanity, but it will eventually teach your Pom that the particular activity is really not all that horrible.

BRUSHING

- Never brush a dog who's dry.
- Never brush a dog who's wet.

Confused? That's understandable.

But when you think about it, both statements really make sense. If you brush your Pom when he's dry, you run the risk of pulling hair out with the dirt. If you brush your Pom when he's wet, his hair is more fragile and susceptible to stretching and breaking.

Ideally, you should brush your Pom when he's damp, either from a bath or by being lightly sprayed with a leave-in conditioner, or after being liberally dusted with a dry shampoo or baby powder.

Brush your Pom at least every other day, a process that will take about ten minutes.

How to Brush

Start with your dog belly up, either on the table or in your lap. Yes, he will need to get used to this position. Tell him what a wonderful boy he is. (If needed, keep the sessions short so that you don't become engaged in a full-fledged war.) Put a towel bunched under him to give him a bit more security.

Brush him out from the bottom up, belly and legs first, using the soft pin brush on his belly and the slicker on the rest of his body. Start out underneath your dog because otherwise it's far too easy to miss the small tangles, ending up with a dog who is smooth on top and tangled underneath—not a good thing. Your buddy's coat grows away from his body naturally, which is why he looks like a dandelion. Brush him in the direction in which his coat grows. Once your Pom gets the idea, he should enjoy this and find it relaxing.

Tangles happen. They happen to dogs with big bushy coats and short scruffy coats and everything in between. The idea is to catch tangles early, when they aren't a big deal.

- **Method One:** The loosest part of a tangle is at its bottom, so try loosening it from the bottom up. When you dig your brush into the top of a tangle and yank, you are actually tightening the tangle and will pull out more hair that way.

It's more effective to work your way upward. You can either use an undercoat rake or a slicker brush for this.

- **Method Two:** First separate the tangle as much as you can by hand. Then use the undercoat rake to pick out the rest. Take your time. Then brush the area out to make sure that you have gotten it all.

A note here about combs: Metal combs work well when checking for tangles, but they don't eliminate them well. In fact, they pull extra

Metal combs are good for checking for tangles; however, they don't effectively eliminate tangles.

hair out and will leave your Pomeranian plotting revenge. Only loosen tangles with a slicker brush or undercoat rake.

BATHING

How often should you bathe your Pom? Well, it depends on your dog. Some Poms have sensitive skin and are prone to

allergies; such dogs should be bathed more often. You can also occasionally use a dry shampoo or baby powder if you have a forced blow-dryer. Sprinkle the powder in generously, leave it in for a few minutes, and then blow it out. Otherwise, only bathe your buddy when he needs it, such as when he's stinky or very dirty or your mother-in-law is coming.

A note about bathing and the ears: Never fill the ear canal with water. Fungus can easily grow in such a dark, wet environment. Before you start the bath, squirt a small amount of witch hazel or hydrogen peroxide into each ear and follow up with a small amount of cotton wool. This will go a long way toward keeping the ears healthy and fungi-free. When the bath is over and you remove the cotton wool, clean the exterior portions of the ear that you can see with a cotton ball. Never insert anything into the ear canal.

How to Bathe

Yes, you can bathe your Pom in the bathtub, but why kill your back when you can use the kitchen sink? A hose attachment is very helpful for this, but a large plastic cup to pour water over your Pom at the proper angle will also do the trick.

Wet your buddy down to the skin and then put the shampoo first in your hand and then on your dog; you'll have better control that way. Move the shampoo straight down the hair. Don't scrub in the shampoo because that will cause tangles. Then, be sure to rinse out the shampoo thoroughly—residue left in the coat after bathing can dull your Pom's coat and will make his skin itchy. Use a wet soapy washrag on his face, feet, and outer part of his ears.

Always use a conditioner after you've completely rinsed the shampoo out of the coat, and don't be stingy, especially if your dog's hair is tangled. It's very helpful to have the conditioner sit in his coat for at least five minutes. Stand by

Although you can bathe your Pom in the bathtub, consider the sink, which is much easier on your back.

the sink to make sure that there's no break for freedom. Rinse the conditioner briefly, but leave the hair a bit slick.

Next, grab two towels. Use one towel to dry him by moving it over his hair in a downward direction, just like you did with the shampoo. Then wrap him in a fresh towel and put him in his crate to dry further for roughly 20 minutes.

Now what? Well, you can hear your Pom shaking vigorously, turning around in his crate, shaking again, and rubbing his head dry against the towel. When he is no longer dripping, you can blow-dry him on a low-heat setting.

A Little Posterior Note

If your dog is sliding along on his butt like he is trying to scratch an itch, his anal glands could be impacted. These glands are easy to express, and the best time to do it is right after a bath. Place your thumb and forefinger on each side of your Pom's anus and press gently. A smelly liquid may come out; you'll almost be able to hear your relieved dog saying "Ahh." If he is still itchy "back there," he may have worms. (Read more about this in Chapter 6.)

Blow-Drying

Your Pom should be blown-out after every bath. If you let a Pom air-dry, his woolly undercoat will mat up, with disastrous results. You're ready to begin once he is no longer dripping and standing on a nonslip surface.

1. Blow-dry and brush the coat, using a slicker brush, from the bottom up, just like when you were brushing your Pom.
2. Once his belly and legs are dry and tangle-free, continue blow-drying him from the top down.
3. Really get under the topcoat to dry the undercoat down to the skin, and watch out for areas like behind the ears and on the cheeks and neck where the hair is extra thick. Close to the skin, make absolutely sure that you get the

undercoat separated and all tangles out. The guard hairs will hold the undercoat separate and maintain the all-important air pockets close to the skin.

4. If you are really going all out for the dandelion look, follow the trick of show handlers. When still damp, massage some gel or hairspray at the base of your Pom's coat. Blow out as usual and his naturally great puffball look will last and last.

Even your mother-in-law will be proud!

After trimming your Pom's feet, do a final trim with the scissors around the edge of the foot for a nice, neat appearance.

HAIR TRIMMING

The goal of trimming a Pomeranian is to make him look like his hair just happened to grow that way. Even show Pomeranians are trimmed very little—basically, you just want to neaten the package and remove stray hairs.

The sound and feel of the clippers can be frightening for your dog. They make a strange noise, and they tickle. To get him accustomed to them, place the tool on your dog's back, business end away from him. Let him feel the vibration as well as hear the noise. Give him treats as you do this to help him associate the clippers with something he loves. (And make sure that your clippers are made for dogs, not people; as previously mentioned, human clippers have a high-pitched whine that annoys most dogs.)

Once your Pom is accustomed to the clippers, take your time when trimming his hair and do a little bit at a time so as not to frighten him.

Feet

Starting with his front feet, trim the hair between his toes and the small bit behind his foot. On his front feet, there is a knob in back; trim up to that. On the back feet, just trim between the pads. Once done with trimming his feet, run your scissors around the edge of his foot to make a neat package.

Tail Hair

Trim carefully with scissors right around the anus to keep this sensitive area clear.

EAR CARE

Poms have prick ears, which naturally stay much cleaner than a drop ear. Still, if not cared for properly, your Pomeranian's ears can become infected and he could go deaf.

HOW TO CARE FOR THE EARS

Fungus grows well in the ear canals, especially when the ears are also wet. So before you start a bath, squirt a small amount of witch hazel or hydrogen peroxide into each ear and follow up with a small amount of cotton wool. This also prevents ear mite (small spiders that like to live in dog ears) infestations. Remove the cotton wool after your Pom's bath.

EYE CARE

A Pom's eyes tear easily and are susceptible to infection. This breed has medium, slightly almond-shaped eyes that are fairly prominent in his small face.

HOW TO CARE FOR THE EYES

Eye care is very simple but needs to be consistent. Check daily for discharge, and remove debris as needed with a warm, wet washcloth.

A Pom's prick ears will stay cleaner than drop ears, but proper care is still necessary to prevent ear infections and mites.

NAIL CARE

Because of their strong desire to please, a Pom is usually more easygoing about nail care than other small breeds, but that doesn't mean that they love it. The trick is to clip a little bit at a time but to be regular about it. This will make nail trimming a tolerated routine rather than an occasional wrestling match. Basically, you don't want to be able to hear your Pom's nails clicking on the floor. That tap dance means that his nails are pushing his foot up and backward as he walks.

If your Pom has decided to make nail trimming his last stand, put him in a soft nylon muzzle, which will click behind his neck and won't restrict his breathing. This type of muzzle will just make it impossible for him to bite you.

HOW TO TRIM THE NAILS

Trim your Pom's toenail where it curves, right below the "quick," the blood vessel that runs down the middle of his nail. Using the big-sized scissors-type nail clippers, cut the nail at the curve or a bit above and always at an angle toward the dog. If you nip the quick, you will make your dog's toenail bleed, but understand that if this occurs, you don't need to head for the emergency room. Just apply some styptic powder, cornstarch, or baby powder to the nail to stop the bleeding.

Dog Tale

Janet Valkowitz writes: "Rascal is a great buddy in many ways, but he hated to have his nails trimmed. He would start howling in 'pain' upon seeing the clippers, long before I even touched him. The whole procedure would leave us both wringing wet and trembling. I tried various things but nothing worked. One day I was leaning back amid a particularly vigorous session, just plain tired. I yawned. Rascal looked up at me, surprised—and stopped howling. I yawned at him again, this time on purpose. Rascal's ears pricked up. I picked up a paw gently and clipped one nail. No screaming! Eureka! I told Rascal he was the best, the most wonderful, the most perfect dog that had ever lived and ended the session.

Rascal didn't get better right away, but yawning got his attention for long enough to convince him that trimming his nails wasn't the torture session he had imagined it to be. He never enjoyed the operation, but he eventually learned to accept it as the mildly unpleasant procedure it was."

Poms do not have naturally healthy teeth, but proper daily dental care can help prevent gum and heart disease.

DENTAL CARE

Some breeds naturally have healthy teeth, but unfortunately, Poms aren't one of them. A Pom's jaw has been miniaturized, but his teeth are still the same size as his bigger spitz cousins. This fosters overcrowding, which leads to an increased incidence of dental disease and eventual tooth loss. Also, a medical connection between gum health and heart health has been found: Unchecked periodontal disease has been linked to cardiomyopathy, a life-threatening condition.

Daily dental care makes a big difference, and yes, I'm talking about brushing your Pom's teeth. There are lots of canine toothbrushes and even specialized brushes that fit on the end of your finger. Toothpaste must always be intended for dogs—human toothpaste will upset your Pom's stomach. It also foams way too much and is difficult to rinse out of the mouth.

Your dog will probably also require regular teeth cleanings at the vet. Consult her as to how often this should occur. If possible, try to find a vet who performs routine cleanings without anesthesia.

HOW TO BRUSH THE TEETH

Does your Pom sit and stay on command? If so, good owner! You are already ahead of the game. If not, review the training instructions in Chapter 7.

1. Start at the top back; put on a small amount of toothpaste on the brush and brush the teeth as you would your own, using a circular motion and making sure to brush to the gum line. Dogs don't need to have their teeth brushed on the inside, so just concentrate on the outside.
2. Brush the bottom teeth in the same fashion.
3. Keep sessions short and happy. You will train your Pom to tolerate this much better if you stop before it becomes a wrestling match.

DEVELOPMENTS IN DENTAL CARE

There are a couple of new developments in canine dental care:

- **Laser teeth cleaning.** Laser cleaning is much more precise than a standard cleaning, which is done by scraping your Pom's teeth. Some vet techs are so good at this that they can do it without anesthesia. Ask your vet if she performs laser cleaning. Any time you can do such a procedure without the considerable risk of anesthesia, you are ahead of the game.
- **Dental additives.** Some products keep a dog's teeth clean with special additives to his food or water.
- **Chew products.** Quite a few treats and bones on the market are designed to help reduce tartar.

FINDING A PROFESSIONAL GROOMER

Although Poms are relatively easy to groom, you may still want some professional help with his grooming.

HOW TO FIND A GROOMER

Ask for recommendations from reputable sources, such as your breeder, your vet, and other Pom owners. Sometimes breeders are also groomers—if this is

If your Pom sits and stays on command, brushing his teeth will be so much easier!

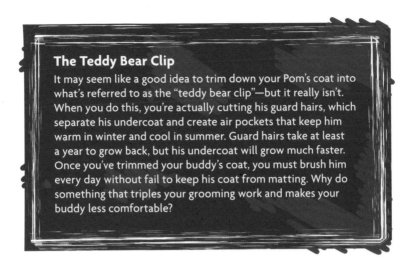

The Teddy Bear Clip

It may seem like a good idea to trim down your Pom's coat into what's referred to as the "teddy bear clip"—but it really isn't. When you do this, you're actually cutting his guard hairs, which separate his undercoat and create air pockets that keep him warm in winter and cool in summer. Guard hairs take at least a year to grow back, but his undercoat will grow much faster. Once you've trimmed your buddy's coat, you must brush him every day without fail to keep his coat from matting. Why do something that triples your grooming work and makes your buddy less comfortable?

your breeder, lucky you! Otherwise, look online to find well-reviewed groomers in your area.

WHAT TO ASK A GROOMER

For the first visit, you won't need to bring your Pom, but you should bring a list of questions for the groomer:

- What are her qualifications?
- What experience does she have with Poms?
- Are her facilities spotless?
- Do the dogs look calm, well cared for, and nicely groomed?

CHAPTER 6

HEALTH OF YOUR
POMERANIAN

A re purebred dogs inherently less healthy than their mixed breed counterparts? That certainly seems to be the current fashionable theory, but let's consider it a bit further.

Genetics form the building blocks of any creature, be it a squirrel, a dog, or a human. When genetics mix in an unlucky combination, they can produce an unhappy medical condition. That's normal with all living things; the trouble comes when an unknowing or uncaring breeder puts two animals together that are carriers or that are exhibiting a medical condition, locking it in and producing the condition in a much higher concentration in their offspring. This can occur with a mixed breed or with purebred dogs.

The key to responsible breeding is the testing of all stock to increase awareness of potential conditions. Only then do you see a reduction in genetic difficulties. When seeking a healthy Pom, your best bet is a breeder who regularly tests her stock and is rigorous in eliminating questionable dogs from her program. Most breeders generally do not make their living from selling puppies and so do not constantly have puppies available. You may have to go on a waiting list, but a bit of a wait is worth it to ensure that you are getting a healthy companion for the next ten to fifteen years.

By far the biggest factor in predicting the good health of your Pom is *you*.

POMERANIAN

72

The care you give him, making sure that he gets the right food, enough exercise, regular dental cleanings, and quality veterinary care, goes much farther than any other single factor in ensuring that he has a long and healthy life.

FINDING A VET

You just brought your puppy home. Now you'll need a vet. Searching for a quality veterinarian should be at the top of your "to-do" list. Above all, you need a vet who has experience working with small dogs. Our little guys require special care, and small dogs commonly suffer from certain health conditions, such as hyperthyroidism and patellar luxation, that a small dog expert will know to watch out for. Your Pom's vet must have a broad knowledge of the symptoms and treatments of these and other small dog diseases. If you live close to your puppy's breeder, ask her for a recommendation. Most responsible breeders are aware of the good vets in their area—and they also know who to avoid. Failing that, friends or neighbors can be a helpful resource.

Evaluate a potential vet on the following traits:

- **Training:** She should of course be a graduate of vet school and possibly also have specialty training.
- **Experience:** Does she see a lot of small dogs in her practice? That's vital.
- **Personality:** Is she compassionate about the health and happiness of your dog? Or does she phone it in?
- **Partnership:** A good vet understands that she needs to work in partnership with you. She includes you in her decisions, letting you know at all times why she is doing what she is doing.

Small dogs commonly suffer from certain health conditions. Your veterinarian should have experience with their symptoms and treatments.

EMERGENCY VETS

If you run into trouble outside of office hours, you will have to take your Pom to an emergency clinic. Just like regular vets, their quality can vary. But you can't interview most emergency vets, as they tend to work on rotating shifts and work odd hours. The clinics change personnel frequently, often using newly trained personnel fresh out of vet school. Don't worry, though—these young vets are often up on the very latest technology and treatments. So how do you tell what's a good clinic?

Before any emergency, ask your breeder which local clinics she recommends. Your regular vet is a good source of this information as well. Also, visit the emergency clinics on your shortlist. Tell the desk personnel why you are there, and check out the facility's general organization and wait times. It'll be pretty obvious if they are caring and well organized.

THE ANNUAL VET VISIT

It seems so automatic. Another year has gone by and your Pom needs his shots. Recently, though, a revolution in canine vaccine protocols has occurred. Many vet schools, the American Veterinarian Medical Association (AVMA), and the American Veterinary Hospital Association (AVHA) agree: Your dog doesn't need vaccinations every year (with the exception of the rabies vaccine, which your town and state governs).

However, just like the regular wellness check we humans receive, your Pom requires a thorough yearly checkup. This will help catch health issues early, before they become big problems, and in some cases may help you make nutritional and lifestyle changes for your Pom rather than treat him with medications. An annual visit not only extends the life of your Pom, but it can

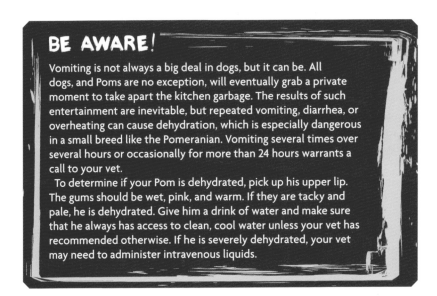

BE AWARE!

Vomiting is not always a big deal in dogs, but it can be. All dogs, and Poms are no exception, will eventually grab a private moment to take apart the kitchen garbage. The results of such entertainment are inevitable, but repeated vomiting, diarrhea, or overheating can cause dehydration, which is especially dangerous in a small breed like the Pomeranian. Vomiting several times over several hours or occasionally for more than 24 hours warrants a call to your vet.

To determine if your Pom is dehydrated, pick up his upper lip. The gums should be wet, pink, and warm. If they are tacky and pale, he is dehydrated. Give him a drink of water and make sure that he always has access to clean, cool water unless your vet has recommended otherwise. If he is severely dehydrated, your vet may need to administer intravenous liquids.

To determine if your Pom is dehydrated, pick up his upper lip. The gums should be wet, pink, and warm.

also actually save you money in the long run.

At the yearly exam, your vet will check your Pom's heart and knees, peer into his eyes, look down his throat, check his stool, and perform a heartworm test. She will also evaluate his general condition, coat, and weight.

PET INSURANCE

Veterinary medicine has become much more effective. Conditions that until recently would earn you a solemn shake of the head can now often be treated. The problem, though, is that the cost tends to be quite high. For example, chemotherapy treatment for cancer can cost thousands of dollars.

For some people, pet insurance, which basically works like human health insurance, makes all the difference. You pay regular premiums, and if your pet gets sick with certain conditions covered by the policy, the company pays your vet bill after you've met a deductible. Plans vary widely, so parse the fine print to avoid a shock at the emergency vet clinic.

VACCINATIONS

Back in the day, and really not as far back as you'd think, rabies, distemper, and parvovirus could kill dogs in a matter of days. Parvo, for instance, was a major killer into the 1980s. As vaccines came along and changed the health landscape, these former death sentences were reduced to the mild inconvenience of a quick prick on a regular schedule.

How often to administer these vaccines has been the subject of several recent studies. The problem is that while vaccines are vital to the health of your Pom, overvaccination can be harmful as well, causing a compromised immune system which is then left open to other conditions. Some vets heavily resisted changes to vaccination schedules because it was considered much easier to get owners to bring their dogs in for yearly shots rather than a yearly "wellness exam," but even the most conservative practitioners are coming around.

HOW VACCINES WORK

Vaccines don't directly protect against a disease; rather, they tease a body into producing antibodies, which then build up protection. This can take up to 15 days, during which your Pom's immune system is a bit compromised. That's why it's not a good idea to give a puppy his shots and then travel the next day.

As long as his dam is feeding him, a puppy carries his mother's immunity—her antibodies will render vaccines ineffective. Shots given before eight weeks or before weaning tend to be at best a waste of money and can actually make your Pom sick. There's no way to tell exactly when the mother's antibodies will start to fade and the vaccination's antibodies will kick in, which is why your Pom is given a series of shots, generally starting at eight weeks. Because his immunity will be questionable before the series ends, your Pom should not have broad interaction with the world around him before four months of age.

Senior Poms may not need as much coverage as their junior counterparts. A senior is less active and goes out less frequently, and he may also already have a somewhat compromised immune system, which could be stressed by vaccinations. Many states now allow most vaccinations to be waived if a sufficient titer count (that is, the sum of antibodies to a certain disease in the blood) is present.

Wait until your Pom is eight weeks old before starting vaccinations. Before then, the mother's antibodies will render them ineffective.

DISEASES TO VACCINATE AGAINST

Dogs can be vaccinated against core and non-core vaccines. Core vaccines are vital to the health of your Pom, while non-core shots are needed only in special circumstances.

Core

Core vaccines protect against the following diseases:
- **Distemper:** This often-fatal viral disease causes high fevers and gastrointestinal

and respiratory inflammation, sometimes with neurological complications.

- **Adenovirus:** This family of viruses causes respiratory and GI-tract infections, as well as pink eye.
- **Parvovirus:** This often-fatal viral disease is marked by fever and diarrhea.
- **Rabies:** This viral disease, spread through the saliva of infected animals, is fatal if it reaches the brain.

The distemper, adenovirus, and parvovirus vaccines are generally administered in combination; they are given in a set of three, paced four weeks apart. The rabies vaccine should be given after 16 weeks, followed by a 3-year booster the following year. A final vaccination for parvo, adenovirus, and distemper should be given sometime after six months. Your Pom shouldn't be given a booster for these more often than every three years unless he is at risk of exposure.

Non-Core

Non-core vaccines include:

- **Bordetella:** Also known as kennel cough, a mild upper respiratory disease caused by exposure to affected dogs.
- **Coronavirus:** This virus causes mild gastrointestinal disease.
- **Leptospirosis:** This serious but rare condition is caused by contact with rats, squirrels, or raccoons.

Senior Poms may not require the vaccination coverage of their younger counterparts.

Poms who frequent the dog park may benefit from the bordetella vaccine.

- **Lyme disease:** This acute inflammatory disease is caused by deer tick bites and is characterized by a rash and inflamed joints.

Does your dog need non-core vaccinations? If he attends doggy daycare or enjoys a romp in the dog park, he will be in regular contact with strange dogs and may benefit from a bordetella shot, but realize that this injection must be administered every six months.

Some areas are at higher risk than others for Lyme disease or coronavirus. Discuss this with your vet. Leptospirosis, also called the rat catcher's disease, is more common in wet, hot climates. Only dogs who regularly hunt vermin are at risk for lepto, and this particular vaccine sometimes causes adverse reactions, so discuss your alternatives with your vet.

NEUTERING

Spaying removes a female dog's uterus and ovaries. Castration removes a male dog's testicles. Neutering is highly recommended for all pet Poms. Unless you plan to become an expert, leave breeding to the professionals, who understand the risks of breeding and whelping. Breeding may seem like a fun endeavor, but if you don't know what you are doing, you are risking your pet's life.

Neutering can pose some long-term health risks if performed before a Pom is seven months old. Also, Poms often have retained baby teeth, and extraction requires anesthesia. Rather than putting your Pom under twice, it's better to wait until he or she has adult teeth coming in before neutering. That way, both procedures can be accomplished in one operation. Poms who weigh less than 4 pounds (2 kg) shouldn't have any elective surgery until they are fully mature—at least a year old—and your tiny female Pom should have at least one season before being spayed. The effects of anesthesia on tiny, immature bodies can be dicey.

Your vet will usually recommend that you neuter your Pom between seven and nine months of age. Discuss your options with her.

BENEFITS

Most people know that pets should be neutered. But what are the benefits exactly? Besides the obvious, that you will not be contributing to pet overpopulation, neutering eliminates any possibility of testicular, uterine, and/or ovarian cancer. Some evidence indicates that males can become less aggressive and will mark their territory less frequently, especially if they are neutered when young.

RISKS

It's wise to be aware of the risks in any activity. Neutering carries the following risks:

• Poms, like all small dogs, are more susceptible to anesthetic complications than their big cousins. It's definitely a good idea to use a vet who is very familiar with small dog surgery.
• Adverse reactions to vaccinations are more common in neutered dogs.
• Neutered males have an increased risk for pancreatitis.
• Strong anecdotal evidence suggests that neutering increases the tendency toward obesity and urinary incontinence, especially in females.
• Some evidence suggests that spaying decreases canine life expectancy. In December 2009, a study published in the journal *Aging Cell* found that Rottweilers spayed after they were 6 years old were 4.6 times as likely to reach the age of 13 as those who were spayed at a younger age.

Risks increase incrementally if Poms are neutered before sexual maturity. Because their hormones never had a chance to grow the body properly, bone and hair loss may occur. Puppies neutered too early may exhibit immature, spindly legs and a permanently adolescent attitude.

PARASITES

The word "parasites" describes plants or animals that live off—or in—another creature. External parasites include fleas and ticks; internal parasites may be anything from various worms to one-celled creatures that can wreak havoc on your Pom's gut. Parasites may infest your dog no matter how careful you are. In warm parts of the country, especially, it's almost impossible to avoid them entirely.

Check for fleas by examining your Pom's coat. Common areas include the armpits, behind the ears, and under the tail.

FLEAS AND TICKS

Fleas and ticks will not just damage your Pom's coat—they also cause health problems. Fleas can carry tapeworm larvae, while ticks can carry Lyme disease. Treat your dog monthly with a collar, spot-on product, or internal pill, and follow the directions on the package.

If you see what looks like little bits of dirt in your Pom's coat, it's probably flea residue. Check for live fleas by examining your Pom's coat, especially behind the ears, in his armpits, and under his tail. If you find any, spray them with a natural flea spray, but know that if you see one flea, there are probably quite a few hiding nearby. A monthly flea preventive will either reduce or entirely eliminate the problem.

There are two ways to remove a tick safely. When doing so, don surgical gloves because you don't know if the tick carries Lyme disease.

- **Method 1:** If the tick is in an area where your Pom's hair is no longer than 1 or 2 inches (2.5 or 5 cm), rub the tick rapidly in a circular motion. After about a minute or two, the tick will back out of your dog's skin and you can dispose of it, preferably down the toilet.
- **Method 2:** If the tick is attached where your Pom has long hair, a rapid circular motion will cause nothing but tangles. Take a pair of tweezers. Grab hold of the tick as close to the skin as you can manage and pull it straight out. Then drop the tweezers in alcohol to sterilize them. Dispose of the tick as above.

If you think that the tick might have Lyme disease (because you live around lots of deer or you are in an area where the disease is prevalent), drop the tick in a jar, close it, and take it to your vet to be checked. Remember that Lyme disease is simple to take care of with a round of antibiotics, but only if you catch it early.

POMERANIAN

HEARTWORMS

Even with a big bushy coat, your Pom will eventually get bitten by a mosquito, and in most areas of the United States, mosquitoes carry heartworm larvae. These migrate from the insect to your Pom when the mosquito feeds. Once in your Pom, the larvae move through the bloodstream to his heart, where they can grow to an impressive length. Untreated, they are fatal. Treatment is draconian, not always available, and not always effective. Prevention is far better: a monthly medication containing ivermectin, which kills the larvae before they can reach the heart.

TAPEWORMS, WHIPWORMS, PINWORMS, AND ROUNDWORMS

A standard part of any wellness exam is a stool check for worms, specifically tapeworms (which come from fleas and have short, flat segments resembling small pieces of tape), whipworms, pinworms, and roundworms. If tapeworms are present, your vet will give you a prescription that contains the active ingredient praziquantel.

Pinworms, roundworms, and whipworms are small nematode worms that infest and live off the contents of the intestines and rectum. If your vet doesn't find any evidence of these worms in your dog's stool, you are good to go, right? Not so fast. These worms are also present in our own systems, so the Centers for

Disease Control and Prevention (CDC) has performed studies on them and found that while the populations can greatly be reduced with preventive treatment, they can never be totally eliminated. Such worms bring down the general health of your Pom and open him up to other illnesses. Stress causes the worms to "drop," or manifest. This is why your Pom gets an upset stomach about three days into a trip. The best way to keep the population down is to treat him on a monthly basis with a fenbendazole product—ask your vet for more details.

Because treatment options are limited, heartworm prevention is highly recommended.

SMALL DOG-SPECIFIC ILLNESSES

No one can deny the cute factor of the under-10-pound (4.5-kg) set. However, whether a Papillon, a toy Poodle, or a Pomeranian, these super minis also share a tendency toward certain health difficulties that are more related to size than to genetics. All small dog owners should keep an extra eye out for the following illnesses.

BLADDER STONES

If your Pom suddenly seems to need to urinate all the time and especially if he is having trouble going, or if he has bloody or smelly urine, he may have bladder stones. X-rays or an ultrasound will tell the tale.

These stones usually comprise the chemical compound calcium oxalate in a Pomeranian and can be formed anywhere in his urinary tract. They're frequently seen in middle-aged to senior Pomeranians, and while some evidence suggests that the condition runs in families, it is highly influenced by your Pom's diet. This is yet another reason why it's a good idea not to feed your buddy table scraps! A healthy, well-balanced diet accompanied by plenty of water is usually all that's needed to keep your Pom bladder stone-free.

If your Pom is diagnosed with bladder stones, he may need a prescription diet (purchased from your vet), which is intended to lower the risk of further stone growth. These diets are often less palatable than your Pom's regular food. If he won't eat his fancy (and usually very pricy) kibble, ask your vet for homemade recipes that your buddy may accept. If the stones get too big and cause a blockage, they may need to be surgically removed.

CARDIOMYOPATHY

Some breeds are more susceptible to heart conditions than others, and unfortunately, Pomeranians are one of them. If your dog is diagnosed with heart trouble, he will be put on a special diet and you will need to ensure that he also gets plenty of mild exercise. Just like with Uncle Ed who has a bad heart but loves triple pounders with fries, you will need to watch your Pom's treats.

One highly effective way to prevent your Pom from developing a heart condition is to make sure that he keeps his teeth clean, as periodontal disease has been linked to heart disease.

COLLAPSED TRACHEA

Collapsed trachea is a serious condition in which the trachea (the tube between the mouth and the lungs) collapses, flattening like a straw that's sucked on too hard. During an episode, your Pom will have trouble breathing, and he will cough reflexively with a noise resembling a goose honk to open his airway. If the cough is one or two explosive outbursts and occurs chronically, he probably has a collapsed trachea.

This condition can be treated short-term with steroids; over the long term, weight loss and the use of a harness instead of a collar (which can compress the airway) are recommended. A cool mist humidifier next to your Pom's dog bed and herbal cough remedies can help as well. Glucosamine and chondroitin are also indicated, as they will protect and preserve the remaining cartilage.

DENTAL DISEASE

Like all small dogs bred down from their larger cousins, Poms are highly susceptible to periodontal disease. Their teeth just don't fit all that well into that little jaw. The tartar on your Pom's teeth isn't just ugly; it can be dangerous. He can lose his teeth, and tartar-causing periodontal disease can also lead to heart disease.

Have your Pom's teeth cleaned regularly—if you can find a vet who performs laser teeth cleaning without anesthesia, so much the better.

Ensuring clean teeth can reduce the risk of heart disease.

PUPPY POINTER

Because Pomeranians are so susceptible to dental disease, it's important that you brush his teeth daily. Here's how to get your puppy accustomed to the procedure:

1. Rub your finger along your puppy's gum line daily as part of his grooming routine. Continue this until he easily accepts you putting your finger in his mouth.
2. Select a gentle brush that fits on the tip of your finger and a canine tartar-preventing toothpaste.
3. Brush the teeth at a 45-degree angle in a small circular motion, making sure to brush along the gum line as well.

HYPOGLYCEMIA

Hypoglycemia is characterized by a sudden drop in glucose in a dog's system and can occur in stressed or active dogs who weigh less than 4 pounds (2 kg). Puppies are especially susceptible because they have so few fat deposits. Hypoglycemia is also linked to an immature liver and liver shunt. (See section "Liver Shunt.") Symptoms include sudden loss of coordination, sleepiness, lack of appetite, and general weakness. If your active little guy suddenly keels over, you are probably looking at hypoglycemia. Left untreated, it can lead to seizures, loss of consciousness, and death.

The magic number concerning hypoglycemia and puppies is 2 pounds (1 kg). Until your fully weaned puppy is over 2 pounds (1 kg), he should be fed at least every four hours and be given 1/4 teaspoon of high-calorie paste twice a day.

If you suspect that your Pom is having a hypoglycemic episode, rub Karo syrup on his gums. Try to feed him some as well, but don't force him or he could choke. Once he recovers, you can give him a small jar of high-protein baby food. Wrap him well and take him to the vet. He may need intravenous glucose.

HYPOTHYROIDISM

Symptoms of hypothyroidism, a disorder in which the thyroid doesn't produce enough hormones, include lack of a proper coat, thickened skin, and lethargy. These are easily reversible with supplemental or synthetic thyroid hormones, but the condition isn't curable. Unfortunately, hypothyroidism is caused by multiple genetic alleles and thus so far has proved difficult to eradicate entirely.

KERATOCONJUNCTIVITIS SICCA (KVS)

A dog suffering from KVS doesn't produce enough tears. The eyes will often have mucus discharge and appear dull. KVS affects many older small dogs, including Poms. The condition can run in families, be caused by prescription medications, result from an injury, or arise from a combination of these factors. Unlike PRA (see section "Progressive Retinal Atrophy"), this is a manageable condition, usually treated with a special salve. But if untreated, KVS can cause blindness.

LIVER SHUNT

A shunt in a railway yard is a good thing—this switching system bypasses a congested train yard to deliver passengers to the station swiftly. However, when a shunt in the body bypasses a vital organ, trouble occurs. With a liver shunt, the blood is sent around and doesn't flow through the biggest toxin filter in the body: the liver. In animals with portosystemic shunts, the blood bypasses the liver and is diverted to another blood vessel, allowing toxins to circulate unchecked throughout the body.

Look for the following symptoms:

- Small body size for their age (yet another reason why not to buy a so-called "teacup Pomeranian")
- Excessive drinking and frequent urination

Loss of coordination, lack of appetite, sleepiness, and weakness can sometimes indicate hypoglycemia. A trip to the vet could be in order.

A small body size for his age can be an indication of liver shunt.

- Depression, sleepiness, or even seizure activity shortly after eating, caused by ammonia (a poisonous by-product of digestion) going to the brain instead of being cleared out by the liver

Prognosis for a liver shunt depends on its location and severity, as well as when it is found. Congenital shunts are good candidates for surgery if diagnosed early. Otherwise, they must be dealt with medically; the dog is given drugs, which chemically clean the blood. This condition runs in families and is yet again a good reason to deal only with a responsible breeder. Reputable breeders do not breed their super-small stock out of concern of perpetuating conditions like this.

PATELLAR LUXATION

If your small dog lifts up and carries one of his rear legs when playing, he may have patellar luxation, or a slipped knee. Movement of the knee can be to varying degrees, from 1 (patella slightly loose on the knee) to 5 (permanently dislocated). This is a highly manageable condition if the knees are a 1 or 2, especially if you have a quiet household where your Pom will not be jumping a lot. Your breeder should tell you the state of your puppy's knees. A Pom with a luxation of 3 or higher will eventually require surgery. Check with your veterinarian to be sure that a Pom with mildly luxating patellas would be a good match for your household. Vitamin C and glucosamine can help ease the symptoms, and you'll need to keep your Pom lean and give him moderate exercise, especially up gentle hills.

PROGRESSIVE RETINAL ATROPHY (PRA)

One day, your little guy starts running into things, usually toward evening. What's going on? It could be PRA; a veterinary ophthalmologist will be able to tell you for sure. This is a disease in which a dog's retina, the lens at the back of the eye, degenerates, usually causing the dog to go blind. There is no cure for this disease, and all breeds have some susceptibility to this condition. It is genetically inherited but recessively, which means that a dog can be a carrier but not affected. Some lucky breeds have a genetic test that can identify carriers, but unfortunately, the Pomeranian is not one of them.

Reputable, responsible breeders regularly test their breeding stock for PRA. Quality breeders may still produce a dog with PRA, but they work very hard to reduce the occasion by testing their breeding animals and not using susceptible dogs in their breeding program.

REVERSE SNEEZING

Your puppy has been running around at the dog park, chasing the bigger dogs. Suddenly he stops, splays his front legs, lowers his head, and starts gasping. His mouth is almost always closed when this occurs. Is this a life or death situation?

No, not really. Basically, your Pom's pharynx (back of the throat) has gone into a sinus-induced spasm triggered by excitement or vigorous exercise, and it'll calm down in a minute or two. An antihistamine can help by opening up the sinuses. Also, try the following to alleviate the problem:

- Close off his nostrils with your fingers so that he has to breathe through his mouth for a minute.
- Rub his throat.
- If inside, carry him outside.

Vitamin C and glucosamine can help ease the symptoms of patellar luxation.

SEVERE HAIR LOSS SYNDROME

Your puppy may have a profuse baby coat but then never quite grow a proper adult coat (which can also be caused by hypothyroidism—see section), or your older Pom's coat may start to thin, starting from his thighs and buttocks and slowly moving forward. Both conditions are called severe hair loss syndrome or black skin disease. The bad news is that this is incurable, but the good news is that your Pom will remain otherwise healthy.

Dog Tale

Carol Kingsley says "As Tito matured, he started losing his fur around the rear legs and back. Nothing I did made any improvement. I took him to the vet and discovered that it was likely caused by either a thyroid disorder or a hormone imbalance. Since Tito was still 'looking for love in all the wrong places,' the vet suggested neutering hm. This would remove the sex urge that was causing the hormones to fire up. It would also make him less likely to wander about in search of romance. I reluctantly had the procedure done on him, but it went smoothly. Tito's hair has completely grown back, and he is handsome and lively, just as before. He isn't wandering away at every chance. He is still a faithful guard dog and loving companion."

COMPLEMENTARY THERAPIES

A good vet, competent and caring, is worth her weight in gold. However, in some instances alternative treatments can be very helpful, especially when they complement your vet's regimen. She may refer you to practitioners that she recommends, or you can look up the major organizations licensing such practitioners online. Often these alternative therapies are also used on humans. Because there can be important differences in working with dogs, make sure that your alternative practitioner is licensed for canines.

ACUPUNCTURE

An acupuncturist inserts fine needles in specific areas to balance the body's flows of energy. Before you think "Ow!" human patients universally say that this doesn't hurt, that there is sometimes an electrical buzzing or an uncomfortable tickle but no pain. Acupuncture is an ancient Chinese practice with some real success rates in pain management and in curing chronic ailments.

CHIROPRACTIC

Chiropractic therapy manipulates your Pom's spine to alleviate lameness and spinal disease. It is often a viable alternative to surgery. Once your vet has ruled out a tumor or fracture, chiropractic treatment can be used to restore fluid and nerve flow to an injured area, allowing healing to begin.

HERBAL TREATMENTS

Herbal treatments employ plant remedies as a gentle alternative to drugs. For example, alfalfa is used for arthritis and allergies. An informed owner (that's you) can use herbs to treat minor conditions, but be sure to let your vet know of any supplement you are giving your Pom, because it can interact poorly with certain drugs.

HOMEOPATHY

Homeopathy uses a very diluted form of the substance that started a certain illness to jumpstart the body's immune system, getting it to fight off the disease. For example, a dog suffering from diarrhea would receive tiny amounts of a substance that causes diarrhea.

SENIOR DOGS

One day you look up and your Pom has some white on his nose. Luckily, due to good breeding practices and advances in veterinary procedures, your Pom will probably stay spry and vigorous well into his teens. But what changes should you make as your Pom advances into seniorhood?

Pomeranians can benefit from a wide range of alternative treatments, including herbal remedies and acupuncture.

SENIOR TIPS

Senior Poms like things the way they are, and they don't like change. Try to keep his routine the same and change it as little as possible. If you must do something new, recognize that your Pom will probably grouse about this a bit, and that's okay. Make sure that the kids in your household respect his status as Senior Advisor. They need to know that games that your Pom once loved may no longer be fun for him.

A senior Pom is more sensitive to heat and cold, so he needs extra protection from both. His coat will naturally thin as he ages, causing him to lose at least some of his woolly undercoat. Be gentle with your brushing, using a small slicker brush, and put away the undercoat rakes—they will hurt his sensitive skin and he doesn't need them anymore. Only bathe him when absolutely necessary.

COMMON OLDER DOG AILMENTS

Regular wellness checks are more important than ever. Never assume that because your Pom is old, it's fine for him to act dull and lethargic. If he is behaving "off," medical conditions may be lurking in there somewhere. These can often be treated or at least alleviated.

The following are some common older dog ailments.

Symptoms of arthritis include joint swelling and pain, which can manifest as a lack of interest in vigorous exercise.

Keep your senior Pom's routine consistent and comfortable.

ARTHRITIS

Arthritis is a condition in which the cartilage has broken down around the joints, either from an injury, a medical condition, or just in conjunction with the aging process. Symptoms include joint swelling and pain, which manifests as a lack of interest in vigorous exercise or perhaps a surprised squeal if touched in the wrong place. Conservative treatment is much better than aggressive drugs, as these can have aggressive side effects. Such treatments include:

• Weight management and a soft bed
• Walks every other day to keep up mobility
• Carpeted stairs to his favorite bed or furniture
• Supplements like glucosamine (which stimulates the synthesis of cartilage) and chondroitin (which helps shield cartilage from destructive enzymes)
• Herbal supplements and homeopathy

Cancer

Does your Pom have a funny bump or a sore that just won't heal? Maybe he has become grouchy and just won't eat? A trip to the vet is definitely in order, and the diagnosis may be cancer.

Treatment for cancer in dogs is very similar to that in humans. Yes, dogs can receive chemotherapy, but they don't suffer most of the side effects that humans

Canine cognitive dysfunction (CCD) is similar to Alzheimer's disease in humans. Dietary change and environmental enrichment can help.

do and their hair won't fall out. Many cancers in dogs are treatable, and your Pom can enjoy an excellent quality of life for many years post-treatment. Discuss all of your options with your vet or cancer specialist and research the topic online. The most important thing to do when your Pom is diagnosed with cancer is to act quickly; delaying action on a diagnosis can mean that a simple, workable procedure is no longer feasible.

Canine Cognitive Dysfunction (CCD)

Does your senior Pom sometimes act like he doesn't know you? Does he sometimes forget the location of important objects like the toy box? He may have CCD, which is similar to Alzheimer's disease in humans. A recent study at the University of California School of Veterinary Medicine found that out of 69 dogs, 32 percent of the 11-year-old dogs and 100 percent of the 16-year-olds were affected.

The first thing you should do is get a thorough vet check to rule out other possible conditions. If she rules out all other possibilities, then your routine will need to reflect the new reality. Your old boy will need to be under someone's watchful eye or in a safe space at all times, either in a room behind gates or in his crate. But it's not all downhill from here! Any sort of environmental enrichment can help. Try these techniques:

- Teach your buddy some new tricks, especially with hand signals, because his hearing may not be so great.
- Invite another dog over to play for the afternoon to give your dog some added stimulation.
- Consider some dietary changes. Good options for CCD contain antioxidants, enzymes, and omega-3 fatty acids.

In a laboratory study of older dogs over a two-year period, the greatest improvement came from a combination of dietary change and environmental enrichment.

END-OF-LIFE ISSUES

There will come a point in your old buddy's life when whatever old dog condition he has will become too much for him. He will usually stop eating and lose control of his bladder and bowels.

Most dogs and their people know when it's time, and euthanasia can be a painless release from suffering. Hug your dog, thank him, and let him go.

A noble and wonderful thing to do in memory of your beloved dog is to donate in his memory to Pomeranian Rescue (http://www.americanpomeranianclub.org/rescue.htm) or the American Kennel Club's (AKC) Canine Health Foundation (http://www.akcchf.org/).

After having had such a wonderful buddy, you may have decided that the pain of losing him makes it just too hard to have another. But someday soon you may decide that it's time to allow another tiny bundle of cold nose and fluff into your life.

TRAINING YOUR POMERANIAN

Pomeranians can be peerless companions if they are well trained. Your Pom feels that there is only one place in the world for him to be—next to you—but this strong desire to be with you at all times can easily morph into separation anxiety. Your Pomeranian should cheerfully follow directions and not perform his potty functions in the house. He even needs to occasionally stay home by himself. To accomplish this, he must have the most amazing and consistent trainer in the world. Yes, that's you!

Every moment is a training moment for your Pom. If you blow your top at him, you are teaching him to leave when you come in the room. If you give him a command over and over, you are teaching him to ignore you. If you feed him from the table "just this once," you are teaching him to beg. Don't forget: If you teach your dog an incorrect lesson, you'll have to first unteach the wrong lesson and then reteach the correct one. It's much easier to make the effort to train your dog correctly from the beginning.

WHAT IS POSITIVE TRAINING?

Old school training, the idea that you should dominate your dog until he obeyed, could get pretty fierce. With the independent yet sensitive Pomeranian, that method has never worked. Poms need to feel that what you are asking them to do is a great idea and that it was theirs all along.

Screaming at your dog is never okay. On top of being a poor technique, this also teaches your dog not to trust you. "That is not negotiable," which can easily be said in a firm, low tone, is very effective, as is a sharp, low "Ack!" But no yelling, ever (and of course physical punishment is a no-no as well).

Treats can be very helpful for some dogs because these rewards grab their attention and give them incentive. Ideal treats include small biscuits or tiny bits of low-fat hotdog—just make sure that they are not greasy and don't fall apart easily. And a few minutes of playtime after a successful training session provide an excellent, calorie-free reward!

You cannot train all behaviors out of your Pom because some are just part of his personality. For example,

Every moment represents a training opportunity for your Pom.

he will always want to chase squirrels and come along with you wherever you go. In these types of instances, you will need to distract him rather than try to eliminate bad behaviors.

SOCIALIZATION

Socialization is a process by which a dog gradually learns about everything in his environment. Until he is two weeks past his battery of vaccines, his exposure to the world and other strange dogs must be limited, or he might get sick. Full socialization should start somewhere between four and five months of age. But you don't need to hide indoors prior to this point—just follow these tips:

- **Have a puppy party, or two.** After all, everyone wants to see the new baby! Ask visiting humans to take off their shoes, which can carry harmful pathogens, and wash their hands before playing with your puppy. Children should sit on the floor before touching the puppy so that if he wiggles out of their arms, he won't fall far.
- **Go for a drive.** This is a great time to get your Pom used to riding in the car. Put him in his crate, strapped to the backseat. Take him somewhere fun, like a bank drive-thru, which often has dog biscuits on hand.

HOW TO SOCIALIZE

About two weeks after his last vaccinations, your Pom is ready to get out there and learn all about the world. Here are some ways to socialize him:

- **Hang out at a park.** There will be lots of dogs there, even if it's not a dog park.

TRAINING YOUR POMERANIAN

Full socialization should start somewhere between four and five months of age.

(Approach dog parks with caution, though—your dog doesn't know how to behave there yet, and he could also be bowled over by another enthusiastic pet.)

- **Walk around the parking lot of any superstore.** Your Pom will get lots of positive attention!
- **Take walks around your neighborhood.** Only go as far as your puppy is comfortable. If a noise or object frightens him, stop and let him check it out. Be calm and quiet and don't try to "reassure" him. Continue when he feels better.
- **Enroll him in puppy kindergarten.** Puppy kindergarten will show your Pom that other dogs are fine and may even be fun. It also allows you to check out a training facility you may want to attend when your buddy is ready for more formal classes. Most quality obedience clubs have such classes; to find one in your area, start at www.akc.org.

CRATE TRAINING

While we humans can feel claustrophobic in small enclosed spaces, dogs are hardwired as den animals to find comfort in dark and narrow places, like under your bed or at the bottom of a pile of cushions. So crating your Pom is not cruel at all—think of his crate as a bedroom, a safe space where he can get away from it all.

HOW TO CRATE TRAIN

When your Pomeranian can't be with you, he needs to be happy at home. The best way to educate your dog to be safe and happy without you is to crate train him.

Most puppies come to their new owner with this training already started, but you will need to continue the training and reinforce it. Follow these steps:

1. Put the crate on the floor with the door open, and place a treat for your puppy inside. When your Pom goes to get the treat, praise him but don't close the door yet.
2. Take him out to the backyard and play with him until he's really tired. Afterward, put him in his crate with a yummy, long-lasting treat. Close the crate door.
3. Put the crate in a quiet room, and cover the crate door with a pillowcase or dish towel. This signals to your Pom that he no longer needs to be a watchdog and can relax. Once he is comfortable, leave the room. Your puppy will probably sleep now for several hours.
4. When you take your puppy out of the crate after several hours, carry him out to his potty spot. He will be ready to go!
5. At night, exercise your puppy vigorously so that he's really tired. Then put him in his crate. This time, put the crate in your bedroom, next to your bed.

Puppies make noises to get what they want. They will continue to make the noises you respond to. If your Pom barks when he wants to come out of his crate and you let him out immediately, he will bark more the next time. Instead, tell

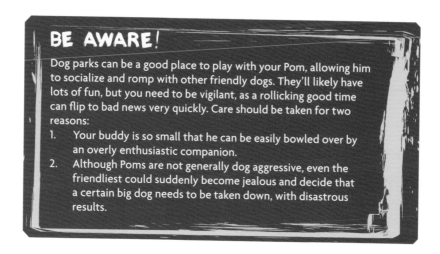

BE AWARE!

Dog parks can be a good place to play with your Pom, allowing him to socialize and romp with other friendly dogs. They'll likely have lots of fun, but you need to be vigilant, as a rollicking good time can flip to bad news very quickly. Care should be taken for two reasons:

1. Your buddy is so small that he can be easily bowled over by an overly enthusiastic companion.
2. Although Poms are not generally dog aggressive, even the friendliest could suddenly become jealous and decide that a certain big dog needs to be taken down, with disastrous results.

your puppy "Be quiet for a minute and I will let you out." When he complies, let him out. This will teach your puppy that not barking gets him what he wants.

Poms are den animals—they find comfort in small, snuggly spaces.

HOUSETRAINING

Some say that big dogs are easier to housetrain than small dogs, but that's not true. They just make bigger messes, so their owners are more motivated to train them.

HOW TO HOUSETRAIN

Done right, potty training is relatively easy.

1. Start with a well-pottied and exercised puppy.
2. Put him in his crate to sleep for three to four hours or for all night, as the case may be. Even if your Pom has to go, because a dog will naturally not want to mess his bed, he will hold it. When you take him from his crate, go with zero detours outside to his "spot." Watch him go and praise, praise, praise.
3. Next, bring him inside and take him to a somewhat restricted area—for example, put a baby gate across the entrance to the kitchen—and hang out with him. You can put down a newspaper or two to catch any possible mistakes.
4. After about a half hour to an hour, he will curl up to go to sleep. Then put him back in his crate and repeat the process.

Young puppies should be taken out first thing in the morning, late morning, mid-afternoon, dinnertime, and right before bed. They also need to go about an hour or two after eating.

This sounds easy, and the steps are actually quite simple, but success requires real commitment. Most puppies take about a month to really get the idea.

HOUSETRAINING ACCIDENTS

As mentioned earlier, yelling at your Pom just convinces him that you are a maniac. Use a low, rumbly phrase like "That is not negotiable" or "You potty OUTSIDE" to make your point, then take him outside. If he has already graduated to whole-house privileges, put him back in the restricted area and go back to keeping an eye on him. He has to regain your trust.

BASIC COMMANDS

A friend called me recently, freshly returned from a trip to Europe.

"You are not going to believe what I saw!"

"What?"

"We went to that posh restaurant you told us about, the one that needs a six-month reservation?"

"Yes! How was it?"

"Amazing, but that's not the point. Several of the guests brought their dogs! There were a couple of Yorkies, a German Shepherd, and even a Pomeranian. They were all quiet as can be. I couldn't believe my eyes!"

The fact of the matter is that dogs often come along with their owners in continental Europe.

It's easy to think "My dog would never behave well enough for that." Well, why not? Are European dogs inherently smarter than American dogs? Nope. In Europe you can take your dog along to many venues, so he must behave. Owners have no choice but to train their dogs!

To be a good companion, your Pom must be able to perform basic commands. All dogs should be able to sit, stay, come, and walk nicely on a leash. They should also follow these commands well all the time, not just when they feel like it. This requires consistent training and practice.

How do you get your Pom's attention? Some like bits of food (low-fat hot dogs or biscuits are good options) and others enjoy playtime with a favorite toy, but all Poms love praise. Be sure to tell your buddy when he has done something right.

Done right, potty training is relatively easy.

You can start with lavish words of approval, but in time a quiet word or two will do the trick. When he doesn't perform a command correctly, your silence will speak volumes.

Don't repeat a command over and over. Saying "COME! COME! COME! COME!" tells your Pom that you aren't sure that he will comply. Far better is to say it once and then try again in a moment, reinforcing him when he complies. That way your dog will know that you mean what you say.

Poms started out as sled dogs, but you don't want him to pull like one! Make his first lesson how to walk nicely on a leash.

Dogs fare far better with several short training sessions than with one marathon. Don't despair if your Pom absolutely refuses to perform a command. Teach the lesson calmly and then leave it alone for that session. You'll find that when you return to it later, some sort of canine lightbulb will have gone off.

WALK NICELY ON LEASH

Poms started out as sled dogs, but you don't want him to pull like one. So make his first lesson how to walk nicely on a leash. You can start this quite young, even before your puppy has all his shots—just be sure to work in your backyard or on a quiet sidewalk, away from other dogs.

Because extra-small dogs like Poms are so easy to pick up, they get carried around so much that you may get the impression that they don't own four legs. If you scoop up your Pom every time he pulls like Nanook of the North or plants all four and refuses to go on, you are teaching him to use these tricks to get a free ride, and he will never learn how to walk nicely on a leash.

When teaching this lesson, you'll need about a 6-foot (2-m) leash. Don't use a retractable leash for training because it won't give you enough control.

How to Teach It
1. To start, place a comfy chair in your yard and bring a good book.
2. Fasten the leash to your Pom's collar. Put him down about 6 feet (2 m) away from the chair, say his name and "Let's go!" and then walk over to your chair.

Use your non-leash hand moving forward in a sweeping motion as the hand signal for this command.

3. Settle into the chair and open to the first page of your book. Your dog will probably watch you resentfully from the other end of the leash, then eventually decide that it's more fun to be next to you.
4. When he comes to you, tell him he is magnificent, wonderful, the best dog ever.
5. Once your Pom comes regularly to your chair, carry him about a short distance up the road from home. Put him down and tell him "Let's go." Dogs like to go home, so this will encourage him to go with you.
6. As he gets good at this over the next few weeks, take him farther away.
7. Begin to walk him away from the house as well as back home. Soon he will be happily trotting around the block with you.

Once he can walk well on a leash, it's time to teach him to walk by your side without pulling on the leash. Walk briskly enough so that your Pom has to work a bit to keep up with you. Pause every once in a while to praise him, but don't talk constantly because he will move away from your side to watch your face to better see what you are saying. Going fast encourages your buddy to hurry to keep up with you. It'll be more fun to keep up with you, and the pulling will lessen.

SIT

Your Pom has started to get the idea of how to walk nicely on a leash. Great! It's time to teach him how to sit on command.

How to Teach It

1. Start with your dog on a small stool or chair, on a leash. (The chair will restrict his movement a bit, and he will be closer to you.)
2. Stand right in front of him, facing him. Take a small morsel of something yummy, raise it above his eyes and then backward above his head, and say "Fido, sit." Raise your index finger as the hand signal for this command.
3. The motion of your hand with the treat will naturally cause him to raise his head and lower his hindquarters to the chair. When he moves into a sitting position, reward him immediately with the treat and praise him.
4. Repeat the exercise two to four times each session. Doing this 3 to 4 times every day will get better results than trying to do 20 times in one go. If your Pom refuses to comply, stop and try again the next day.
5. When your Pom sits well on the stool, put him on the ground and perform the same exercise on the floor.

DOWN

Once your Pom sits easily, you can teach him the *down*.

How to Teach It

1. Put him back on his stool or chair, off the leash.
2. Say "Fido, down." Put a small goodie in front of his nose.
3. Move it downward and slightly forward. His head will follow the goodie and he should slide into a *down*. Move your outstretched hand down as a signal for this.
4. Praise and reward him with the treat when he's completely in the *down*.
5. When your Pom is consistent on the chair, teach him the command on the ground.

Placing your Pom on a chair or stool will restrict his movement while he learns to sit.

STAY

Your puppy has probably already perfected the iconic "Pommie Stare": head back, quietly watching you—but he still needs to know the command so that he'll stay when *you* ask him. When he understands this command, he can politely watch you at the dinner table without begging. He can allow guests to come into the house without jumping on their legs with muddy footprints. You can even save his life! For example, if your Pom ever dashes out the front door and makes a beeline for a busy street full of zooming cars, you can stop him with a "Fido! Stay!"

How to Teach It

1. Fasten the leash on your Pom's collar and place him directly in front and facing you on a small, steady stool or chair.
2. Say "Fido, sit!" Then say "Stay!" Put your hand up in a stopping motion.
3. Wait about a second and then release him with "Good dog!" Release your dog before he has his own bright idea to get up and head out; this will reinforce

the command and encourage the general idea that staying is a good thing.

4. Gradually increase the length of the *stay* command. When your Pom can do it well for ten seconds, back up a bit. When he can stay like that for ten seconds, back up some more, and so on.

5. When his *stay* is steady from several feet (m) away, put him on the ground and repeat the same sequence. Once he can do this, perform the same sequence again but off leash. Of course, always train off-leash work in a secure area.

COME

Like *stay*, *come* is a vital, lifesaving command. The ability to call your Pom back to you when he has become loose can save his life. Of course, he already knows this command—every time he runs to you when you rattle his food bowl, he is responding to the concept of *come*. But he needs to learn how to do this at your command, not just at his own whim.

How to Teach It

1. Once your Pom is steady on his *stay* on the ground but still on a leash, say "Fido, come!" Then back up swiftly. Beckon with your hand as the hand signal for this.

Your Pom should always feel that coming to you is fun.

2. Your curious Pom will want to know what you are doing and will follow you. When he does, praise him.
3. As he gets better at this, increase the distance that he has to come. But always keep it fun, short, and sweet. You can always continue the lesson tomorrow.
4. When your Pom consistently comes on leash, take the leash off and perform the same exercises again. Again, always train off-leash work in a secure area.

Your Pom should always feel that coming to you is a fun. Never use this command to get your dog so that you can correct him for something because he won't want to come anymore.

GETTING PROFESSIONAL HELP

Occasionally, people can get all the training help they need from a book, but most of us require more than that. Obedience classes can keep you motivated and give you a live person to answer your questions. Big-box pet stores often offer classes, and obedience clubs in most cities provide reasonably priced classes from highly experienced trainers. Visit www.akc.org to find a club near you.

You may not be able to find classes near your home. If this is the case, you can also hire a trainer to come to your home. One-on-one sessions are more expensive than classes, but they're also more personalized. You can find a good trainer by asking your breeder or dog-owning neighbors for a recommendation. A good trainer should:

Dog Tale

Lisbeth Cesar writes: "When Rufus was a puppy, we did everything wrong. We picked him up every time he whined, so he cried to get what he wanted. We thought that crate training was cruel, so Rufus was able to wander the house, leaving little puddles behind him. What a mess! It took him nipping my daughter's friend to realize how bad things had become. I called my breeder and she recommended the local AKC obedience club. I didn't see how teaching Rufus to walk next to me was going to help, but my breeder said it was worth a try. First of all, the club showed me how to properly crate train Rufus; that was a huge relief because it meant we could also potty train him. And the general commands worked wonders. I realized that Rufus had never before respected what I was telling him to do. Today he is (goodness knows) not perfect, but he recently received his Canine Good Citizen title—boy were we proud!"

A good trainer should
have experience
working with Poms, or
at least small dogs.

- **Be reputable.** Ask for references from a potential trainer. She should also belong to some sort of professional organization. The Association of Pet Dog Trainers (APDT) has a user-friendly website, www.apdt.com. You can start your search there.
- **Be knowledgeable.** The trainer should know the ins and outs of training small dogs. Harsh training methods will cow your dog, and he will plot revenge. A good trainer will be skillful, with firm but positive training methods.
- **Have experience.** Ideally, you want someone who has worked with lots of Poms, but if this isn't possible, she should have lots of experience working with small dogs.

SOLVING PROBLEMS
WITH YOUR
POMERANIAN

Mimic a yawn to calm down your excited pup.

omeranians are cheerful sprites, bred over the centuries to be the ideal companion. But a Pom's talents don't always fit the modern concept of a quiet canine homebody and couch potato. Even when well trained, a Pom can make a sudden executive decision to bark every time you leave him alone or to tinkle in the back corner of the living room. A savvy Pom owner knows that she needs some specialized methods to deal with the unique situations her mighty mite can get himself into.

PROBLEM-SOLVING TOOLS

Before we begin talking about what to do about specific problems, here are some simple tools to help you problem-solve.

THE POWER OF A GOOD YAWN

Poms can be excitable creatures, and their heritage dictates that life should be lived next to their owners at all times. Any command that doesn't fulfill this need is going to be difficult for them to execute. A simple general tool to relax your dog is what two playing dogs do when their roughhousing gets a bit out of hand: yawn.

One turns his head away from the other, breaking eye contact, licks his lips, and yawns.

If dogs can use this with each other, so can you! It's like a secret dog code!

LEAVE IT

It can be difficult to teach your Pom not to do something. When you tell him that a behavior is wrong or bad, he may just think that you are cranky. He won't connect his behavior to that cat whizzing by or the napkin lying under the table just asking to be shredded.

So how do you teach him not to do something? The key is to turn the lesson into something positive. Try the following *leave it* command:

1. Take a small treat that fits in the palm of your hand.
2. Show your dog your hand with the treat firmly hidden in your fist.
3. Tell him "Leave it." Let him sniff and nudge at your hand.
4. When he leaves your hand alone, give him the treat. Repetition is the key here—perform this exercise several times a day.
5. Then intermittently, whenever you are playing with your dog and giving him treats, hold one tightly in your fist first and tell him, "Leave it." When he leaves your hand alone, give him the treat. This will keep the command fresh in his mind.

Once he is leaving your hand alone, you can train him to leave other items alone, like the smelly socks on the floor or even a dropped chocolate bar.

Use treats to teach your Pom how to be gentle with human friends.

TOUCH IT

Your Pom may get nippy sometimes, even when he isn't being aggressive. He uses his mouth a lot like we use our hands, and he has a much thicker skin than humans do, not to mention all that hair. He knows that to get a fellow dog's attention, he needs to grab pretty hard, so when the friend is human rather than canine, he can be too rough. Here's how to teach your Pom to touch something gently:

1. Say, "Fido, touch it," and invite your Pom to touch your closed hand with a small goodie inside.
2. When he touches your hand, open it and give him the goodie. The idea is for him to not grab at your hand; he only gets the treat when he touches your hand gently.

TRICK TRAINING

Tricks actually possess far more than just entertainment value. Even if you don't intend to turn your Pom into a professional circus dog, tricks are a vital tool to distract him from some behaviors, such as being nervous about thunderstorms or trying to herd quickly moving kids. If he knows a trick or two, you can ask him to perform the trick instead of the poor behavior.

Teaching a trick is actually very easy:

1. First watch your Pom in action—dogs naturally perform cute behavior all day long.
2. When you see your Pom do something cool, name the action.
3. Every time he naturally does the trick, say the name out loud and reward him with a treat.
4. Sooner or later your Pom will connect the action to the name and treat.

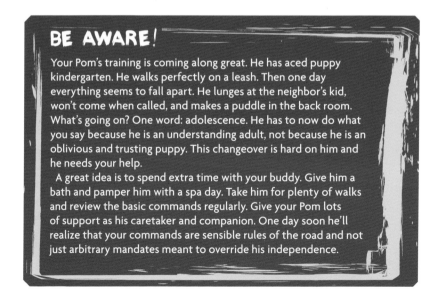

BE AWARE!

Your Pom's training is coming along great. He has aced puppy kindergarten. He walks perfectly on a leash. Then one day everything seems to fall apart. He lunges at the neighbor's kid, won't come when called, and makes a puddle in the back room. What's going on? One word: adolescence. He has to now do what you say because he is an understanding adult, not because he is an oblivious and trusting puppy. This changeover is hard on him and he needs your help.

A great idea is to spend extra time with your buddy. Give him a bath and pamper him with a spa day. Take him for plenty of walks and review the basic commands regularly. Give your Pom lots of support as his caretaker and companion. One day soon he'll realize that your commands are sensible rules of the road and not just arbitrary mandates meant to override his independence.

Then you will be able to say the name of the trick and he will perform it on command.

Once he has several tricks under his belt, you can take your Pom to senior centers or hospitals to entertain people to no end. For more information on this, see "Therapy" in Chapter 9.

PROBLEM BEHAVIORS

Even when you religiously work with your Pom on the basic commands, problems can crop up that require specific solutions. Here are some of the more common difficulties and what to do about them.

HELP! MY POM WON'T STOP BARKING!

Poms can be surprisingly noisy. They'll warn you about intruders, the neighborhood cat, or the kids walking home from the bus stop. Fortunately, you can teach your Pom to keep the noise down.

If there are a lot of people moving in and out of the house for a limited period, it's probably a good idea to put your chatty boy in his crate and cover the door with a sheet or a pillowcase until things quiet down. This is the signal that your mini-doorbell can relax and go off duty.

It may sound counterintuitive, but the best way to teach your Pom to stop barking is to teach him how to bark. Basically, if you can gain control at the start of the action, then you can end it, too.

1. When your Pom barks (at a point in time when it's okay), say, "Fido, bark! Good dog!" to capture the behavior.
2. Then when he barks when you'd like him to stop, say, "No bark! Good dog!" and reward him when he stops barking.

HELP! MY POM WON'T LET ME LEAVE!

Pomeranians know that their place is by your side. Although you can take your dog with you more often than ever before, places like the grocery store or your mother-in-law's house may not welcome him. Poms tend to disagree on this point and can be quite adamant about coming along. If you do not give in to your Pom's demands, he may serenade your neighbors for hours with his tale of woe or quietly dismantle the sofa.

Early and consistent crate training is a must for every Pomeranian. If your Pom cries piteously while in his crate, put him in a quiet, darkened room with the crate covered if necessary. When you must leave him in the crate for a period, give him a yummy bone stuffed with kibble and peanut butter to distract and occupy him.

HELP! MY POM IS CHEWING!

Pomeranians are generally not heavy chewers, but especially as their adult teeth come in, even your buddy can decide that it's fun to take on a kitchen table leg or maybe those yummy-looking electrical cords. How do you dissuade him from this?

1. Put an antichew paste on all potential targets. This can be purchased at any pet store.
2. Fill up your Pom's toy chest with big yummy bones, cloth tug toys, and anything else good to chew. You want your little friend to have plenty of the right stuff to gnaw on.

HELP! MY POM IS DIGGING!

Poms aren't big diggers, but every once in a while they decide that it just might be fun. Usually they start digging because they are bored, and then it becomes a habit. To cure your Pom of this:

1. When you notice a hole in the yard, put a roll of his stool at the bottom.
2. When your Pom goes back to expand on his work, he will quickly decide that he doesn't want to dig there anymore after all.
3. Once you've done this several times, he will look for a different pastime.

Give your Pom more exercise as well—he'll benefit from more interaction with you. High-activity toys like canine puzzle games, where your Pom has to press a certain section to get some kibble, will also alleviate his boredom.

HELP! MY POM ESCAPES OUT THE FRONT DOOR!

You cannot overestimate the deep, gut-wrenching panic that hits when your little guy escapes from the house. This is why it's vital that he have good manners at the front door. Use his well-trained *sit* and *stay* to teach him never to pass through a door before you.

Keep your Pom's walk going after he potties.

Most Poms need to potty twice in quick succession. Taking your dog out a second time can help.

1. Sit your Pom next to you at the door.
2. Say, "Fido, stay!" Then put his leash on him.
3. Go ahead of him through the door.
4. Release him with the command "Let's go!" and let him move through the door.

Everyone in the household must follow this simple drill. After all, what good is it if your Pom minds you but is happy to dash out in front of Grandma? It shouldn't take long to teach him this once he is steady on his *sit* and *stay*.

HELP! MY POM HAS FORGOTTEN HIS HOUSETRAINING!

As mentioned in the last chapter, potty training is pretty simple even though it takes a major commitment on your part. But what do you do if your Pom forgets? You have to go back and retrain the basic rules. However, two areas can be extra troublesome.

Help! My Pom Won't Potty on Lead

It can be seriously annoying to take your Pom out to potty on lead. While you stand there waiting, he sniffs and sniffs until you feel he has made introductions with every blade of grass in the front yard. Impatient and frustrated, you decide that he doesn't really need to go and you take him back inside. Then you turn your back for one minute and he does the deed on your floor. What should you do?

Everything you feel about your Pom communicates down the leash as if it were a telephone wire. If you are in a rush and impatient, tugging him about from place to place, he will definitely react to that. Here's what to do:

1. Find the place where you want your Pom to go, and stop there. Watch the sky overhead. Check out the animal figures in the clouds. Pay as little attention to your Pom as possible. If you relax, your buddy will relax.
2. Once he potties, praise him enthusiastically.
3. Take him for a nice walk.

Never go back inside the second your Pom potties, or you will teach him to hold it as long as possible to extend his time with you. If you follow these steps, your dog will have a regular and happy routine for going out to relieve himself on a leash.

Help! My Pom Potties in the House!

It starts with a funny smell. Following your nose, you find a small yellow ring at the edge of the carpet, smell attached. Before you react, realize that your buddy has long since forgotten the event. If you yell at him now about using the house as his toilet, you will just reinforce his opinion that you are a cranky human, prone to arbitrary outbursts at any time. Instead, your response needs to be more basic:

1. First, restrict your Pom's access to out-of-the-way places in the house. (See "How to Housetrain" in Chapter 7.)
2. If you do bring him or her into the rest of the house, make it only in a belly band (if your dog is male) or doggy britches (if your dog is female). If he lifts a leg or she squats, say, "ACKKK!" and with a low rumble, "You potty OUTSIDE," and take your Pom outside.
3. Conduct a major spring cleaning with an enzymatic cleanser. If you've seen one puddle mark, rest assured there are probably many; an ultraviolet light will tell you for certain. If you have been thinking of changing out a carpet or two, now is an excellent time. Dogs like to go where it smells "good" to them, where they have already pottied and left their scent. Eliminate these spaces and your Pom will be less interested in going there.

Everyone in the house must participate for training to stick.

4. If he doesn't have a backyard to use, his bathroom walks may be too short. Most dogs will go soon after coming outside, play for a while, and then need to go again. You may be missing this second elimination. One way to handle this if you are tight on time is to potty him twice. Take him out the first time and make sure that he potties thoroughly. Come back inside and put him in his crate. After a half hour, take him out again.

HELP! MY POM IS A POGO STICK!

Although a Pom won't generally topple a child by jumping up on her, a dog who mimics a pogo stick can only be annoying, especially when greeting guests. There is a time and a place for jumping. Jumping over obstacles in agility work and even bounding around is fine, but becoming a pogo stick to greet guests at the front door? Not so much.

Beware! If even one person in your household thinks that your Pom's bouncing is darling, the following steps will not work. The training needs to be consistent, and everyone has to participate.

1. Teach your Pom how to sit as outlined in Chapter 7. Dogs learn best with short, frequent training sessions, so over several days, lengthen the length of the sit to about three minutes.

2. When you are sure that your boy can sit for three minutes without the leash, ask a friend to come to the door and knock softly.

3. Tell your dog, now back on the leash, "Sit." Your friend shouldn't even come in the front door until he is steady on his *sit* with this distraction.

4. Once he is steady with the knocking, your friend can come inside. She should be able to say a friendly hello to you without Fido attacking her with joyful bouncing. It is very important when your friend comes that she ignore your dog.

5. When your buddy is steady on his *sit*, even after your friend has greeted you

Dog Tale

Kristina Haggers writes: "I bought a Pom because I loved the idea of having a 'take-along' dog. My Patches was perfect for the first three years and we were inseparable. But then my mom got sick and I was needed to take care of her. At first I left Patches for long hours in her crate. This was obviously not a good idea, so I contacted a doggy daycare to watch her during the day. Patches would growl at the other dogs, and when she bit a caretaker, I had to take her home. I called my breeder in tears. She recommended that I get another relative to help with my mom for a few days. I was to take Patches on some nice long walks and then really pamper her with brushing, bathing, and grooming. This was an especially good idea because Patches had become quite matted. Following this, I was to go to a new doggy daycare with her and hang out there together for several hours. My breeder thought that Patches would accept the place once she saw that I liked it there.

This worked like a charm! Patches has loved that daycare ever since, and sometimes now I drop her off not because I need to but so that she can have a fun day with her friends."

and chatted for a moment, she should reach down and give him a pat.

6. Release your Pom with "Say hello" or even "Give paw" if he has learned this trick. He will be rewarded for being quiet and respectful by the attention your friend showers on him; this will further encourage him to be quiet and respectful. You are done when your Pom is steady on this step several times over several days.

HELP! MY POM GETS NIPPY!

Even though a Pom can't take a chunk out of you like, say, a German Shepherd Dog could, he can still be a real menace. When you treat your Pom like a baby instead of a dog, he can become very demanding, expecting you to be at his beck and call. He may even nip to get his way. *Touch it* can be very helpful in eliminating this behavior because it will teach him to approach without hurting you.

GETTING PROFESSIONAL HELP

Sometimes problem-solving techniques work, and sometimes, despite your best efforts, they don't. If you've tried one or more of the training techniques outlined above and they aren't working, consider the following:

- Look back at the original book or go back to the person where you got the training idea. The question to ask is "Am I doing this right?"
- If you were doing things correctly and it's not working, it's time to change gears.
- If you have changed your gears several times without success, it's time to get help.

Your breeder can often help, and you can search the Internet for answers. But if that isn't enough, you may need a behaviorist. Many big vet practices have one on staff, and if you go to obedience classes, your club may be able to recommend a good one.

A good behaviorist:

- Has experience and a track record of successfully working with small dogs.
- Can get inside your Pom's head and see how he ticks. That's often the key to success.
- Is not slavishly married to any one training method.
- Only uses kind training methods.
- Is willing to listen and work with you. After all, you know more about your Pom than anyone else does.

Don't ever let things get so bad that you seriously consider giving your Pom up for adoption. Owners surrender their dogs every day because of some training or behavioral issue. However, there's real help out there in many shapes and forms. One of them will work for you. You owe it to your buddy to not give up.

A good behaviorist has a successful track record with small dogs and is willing to work with you to help your Pom.

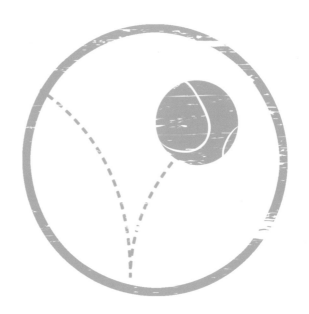

ACTIVITIES WITH YOUR POMERANIAN

The Pomeranian was created to be an out-and-about dog. Independent and confident, he was bred to hang with you, whether you are competing together, doing therapy work, or heading cross-country. They were never made to wait patiently for you to arrive back from the business of life! Poms want to be with you, in the thick of things.

SPORTS AND ACTIVITIES

Pomeranians are well suited for a surprising variety of canine sports. Beneath their pretty puffball coat, they are athletic and light on their toes, able to zig and zag with the best of them. Your Pom will enjoy any sport that requires him to work closely with you.

AGILITY

Think about a timed boot camp obstacle course, and you'll get an idea of what agility is like. Like the human sport parkour, dogs navigate tunnels, negotiate weave poles, walk a balance beam, climb a wall, and jump over a low fence. He needs to be in great shape for this vigorous sport, so check with your vet to make

Poms do quite well at agility, a timed sport in which dogs must navigate an obstacle course.

PUPPY POINTER

Experienced dog trainers have a saying: Let your puppy be a puppy. What does that mean? Your adult Pom will be a better companion—and exhibit better manners too—if you take things slowly. Before he has had his full battery of shots, he has no business being around strange dogs or in lots of public places. But even after that, he's not ready for intensive training. Take your Pom to puppy kindergarten for sure, but let him chill the rest of the time. He can start conformation and obedience training at four to five months of age, but keep sessions short and fun. Your Pom shouldn't start agility training until he's a year old because all that jumping can have a bad effect on growing muscles and bones. When you wait for the right time, your buddy will learn quickly and retain his information easily.

sure that he's ready—his knees must be absolutely sound. You must be fit as well because you'll have to run alongside your buddy to guide him through the course. This is not a sport for the faint of heart, but agility addicts swear that a rollicking good time is had by all.

CANINE FREESTYLE

Canine freestyle (dancing with dogs) is difficult for most Pomeranians. They are so small that it's hard for them to peer up from their low angle to see your facial expression, which allows them to follow your nonverbal cues. This causes them to move farther away from you to get a better vantage point, and not all dances allow for this. Poms have more discipline than many other toy breeds to drill a performance over and over, but in general, this is probably not the best sport for most Poms.

CANINE GOOD CITIZEN® TEST

The Canine Good Citizen is a basic test for canine good manners. Most Poms can pass it easily after they have attended a basic obedience class series or two. During the test, your Pom will be tested on the following:
• accepting a friendly stranger
• sitting politely for petting
• accepting being groomed
• going out for a walk on a loose leash
• walking through a crowd
• sitting down on command

Experienced dog trainers agree: Let your puppy be a puppy. Give your Pom adequate time to grow before training for competitions.

- coming when called
- reacting well to another dog
- reacting well to distraction
- tolerating supervised separation well

Being able to add "CGC" at the end of your dog's name will give you serious bragging rights! But much more importantly, your Pom will possess basic good manners.

CONFORMATION (DOG SHOWS)

Have you ever been to a dog show? Did it sometimes seem like controlled chaos or even a little silly? Well, if you've ever enjoyed looking at a lovely smooth Dachshund or delighted in a goofy, sweet Golden Retriever, you can thank dog shows.

The real purpose of the sport is to uncover the cream, the very best, of a particular breed. An experienced and expert fancier gives her opinion of how well each dog in his ring conforms to the standard of an ideal specimen of that breed. Then the best dogs are used to create future generations. The Pomeranian standard talks about correct Pom temperament, describes what a perfect headpiece and body proportions should look like, and speaks in great detail about the ideal Pomeranian coat. The closer a particular Pomeranian approximates this standard, the better he will fare in conformation.

Showing is much harder than it looks, and it takes real skill and not a small amount of talent. A properly trained and shown Pom is a beautiful miniature statue, stepping out proudly on four perfect little paws.

If you think that you might like to show your Pom, speak to your breeder and attend local dog shows. Go to www.infodog.com for more details, or visit the American Kennel Club's (AKC) website at www.akc.org for available clubs and classes.

OBEDIENCE

If agility is a rollicking line dance, then obedience is a precise quadrille. Your Pom is required to be exact in all his movements, and points are taken off for any lack of finesse.

At the Companion Dog (CD) level, a dog is required to heel quickly or slowly, on or off lead as the judge requires; stand for examination; sit quietly with his owner across the ring; and stay quietly with his owner across the ring for a *down* of several minutes. At the Companion Dog Excellent (CDE) level, the dog must heel off lead, as well as tackle directed jumps. The Utility Dog (UD) level adds scent discrimination; the dog must be able to pick a dumbbell and a glove out of a pile by scent only.

After taking a basic obedience class series, Poms should pass the Canine Good Citizen® test with ease.

Poms can do well in obedience, and several have achieved top honors. However, this breed requires a handler who understands a small dog's need for variety and fun in training. Also, these dogs are so little that they can have a hard time seeing exactly what their handler wants; from their perspective, humans are quite tall, so they may require some extra training.

RALLY

In the sport of rally, a dog and handler navigate a task course set up with a series of signboards in a ring, moving from one numbered sign to the next and performing each activity (like sitting or lying down on command) as directed. The exercises are very similar to those in regular obedience, and dogs progress at roughly the same pace. Poms can excel as well in rally as they do in obedience.

Obedience and rally competitions require precision and finesse. Training should always provide variety and fun.

Rally requires a handler who can easily understand and follow directions—the judge will not tell you what to do in the ring. If you misunderstand one of the signboards, your Pom will lose points. Are you the one with questions after everyone else in a group understands what to do? Do you have trouble following a map on a road trip? Consider these questions when debating whether rally is a good choice for you and your Pom.

THERAPY

Poms have been bred over the last millennia to be cheerful and comforting dogs. A therapy dog's job is to cheer up and comfort people in hospitals, retirement homes, and schools. Sounds like a pretty good match for this breed, and it's true—a well-trained, well-socialized Pomeranian makes an excellent therapy dog. They also possess the magic "aww" factor that can melt the stoniest heart. Poms often reach people who would be intimidated by a more imposing dog.

Elaine Smith, a registered nurse who worked for a time in England, was struck by the response of the patients to a chaplain who made his rounds with a Golden Retriever. Returning to the United States in 1976, Smith started a program to train dogs to visit institutions. Over the years, demand for therapy dogs has continued to grow as their therapeutic value continues to be positively verified.

Pet Partners, one of several organizations that certifies and registers therapy dogs, has a four-step program for interested applicants:

1. Take a training course—that's for you, not your dog.
2. Undergo a vet check.
3. Get evaluated as a team.
4. Submit an application.

With your Pom along for the ride, being a therapy dog team can be very rewarding indeed.

TRAVELING WITH YOUR POM

Small enough to fit almost anywhere, the jovial Pom is the ultimate take-along dog. But you need to bring the correct equipment and follow some sensible rules of the road to travel safely and efficiently. Here are the supplies that will make the difference between a stroll in the park and a disaster waiting to happen.

For all trips:
- large carrying bag
- waste-pickup bags
- walking leash and collar
- water, either bottled or from home

For a trip longer than a day:
- food
- favorite dog toys
- first-aid kit

Dog Tale

Carol Kingsley says, "My rescue Pom, Tito, would sometimes wander from home. He was not neutered when I first got him, so he was always looking for love in the wrong places. Once he got away and I couldn't find him anywhere. Days went by. I was frantic and completely distraught. I had signs up all over town and ads in the newspaper and on the radio. Two weeks went by with no sign of him. Then just when I was accepting that I would never see him again, a lady called me early one morning and said that she might have my dog. I eagerly went to meet her. Miracle of miracles! It was my little Tito. He had been to the groomer and looked well cared for. I was so grateful to have my friend returned!"

• hard-sided plastic crate or soft-sided crate that can be assembled at your destination

TRAVELING BY AIR

As long as your Pom is well crate trained, traveling by air is almost as easy as going by car. Just observe the following tips and equipment suggestions.

Reservations

When you make your airline reservation, say that you want to bring your dog with you. The agent will go over the exact requirements, although you generally won't have to pay for him until check in.

Most airlines have a limit of dogs allowed in-cabin per flight. So make your doggy reservation earlier rather than later. If you plan to change flights, make sure

Poms make excellent therapy dogs. With a certification from Pet Partners, you and your Pom can bring comfort to those in need.

Make flight reservations early to ensure that there's room for your Pom. Observe airline-specific regulations and bring a comfy crate.

that all the airplanes you want to use can accommodate in-cabin dogs. Some planes are just too small.

Health Certificate

Airlines generally don't require travel health certificates for dogs flying in-cabin, but double-check to make sure. Also, if you are traveling overseas, your destination country will certainly want a health certificate and may have other stringent requirements. Check the country's website for more information. Be sure to follow its rules exactly.

Crate

A triangular soft-sided carrier, especially one with wheels, is the best way to go when traveling with your dog in-cabin. These soft-sided carriers allow plenty of airflow with lots of mesh siding, so your dog can breathe easily. The triangular shape means that when the carrier is upright, your Pom can sit up fully. When you lay it on its side, he can stretch out. It has a telescoping handle and wheels so that you can pull it behind you, as well as straps so that you can use it as a backpack. You will need to slide the crate under the seat in front of you.

Bring a hard-sided plastic crate with you too. You can pack it as one of your suitcases. Your Pom will need the security of a regular crate at your destination.

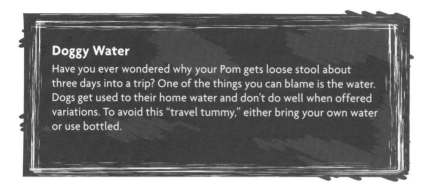

Doggy Water

Have you ever wondered why your Pom gets loose stool about three days into a trip? One of the things you can blame is the water. Dogs get used to their home water and don't do well when offered variations. To avoid this "travel tummy," either bring your own water or use bottled.

The best plastic crates have screws to hold the two sides together.

The Flight

Arrive early to check in with your Pom. Security will want to inspect the in-cabin bag while you carry your buddy through the metal detector. A small note here: Although you pay a handsome extra fee to bring your dog in-cabin, the airplane considers him one of your carry-on bags. Unfair but true!

Most airlines will let people who need a bit of extra time board early. It's smart to take advantage of this. Once you are in your seat, settle your Pom in and then—and this is the most important tip of all—leave him alone. The more you talk to your dog, pat him, reassure him, and check that he is okay, the more you're actually telling him that there is something to worry about. Enjoy your magazine and the view above the clouds. Your Pom may be restless for a bit, but when he can tell that you are unconcerned, he will calmly fall asleep.

TRAVELING BY CAR

Would you let your kids ride in the front seat of the car? Of course not. Neither should your Pom! Put him in his plastic crate, and belt it in the backseat. This is another reason why crate training is so important.

Settle your Pom into his spot, flip on the radio, and head to your destination. He may whine a bit, but he's trying to see if you will respond. Don't! Let him know by your calm attitude that everything is okay.

If for some reason your Pom has decided that he doesn't like car rides, the solution is a gentle acclimation rather than leaving him at home. Do it this way:

1. Sit with your Pom in your parked car for a couple of minutes a couple of times a day until he relaxes—and don't forget to give him treats at the same time.

BE AWARE!

It can be happen so quickly. One second your buddy is asleep at your feet; the next second you answer the door and he slips between your legs after a squirrel—and disappears.

Time is of the essence. If you notice that your dog is gone within a couple of minutes, he probably hasn't gotten that far.

- Go outside and call your dog. He's gotten farther away all alone than he's ever been. He's not so sure of himself.
- When you see him, don't rush him and try to pounce—you will probably scare him. He may run, and even a small dog can get away in a fashion that no human can follow. Instead, calmly tell your Pom to stay, and go over and pick him up. If you had enough presence of mind to pick up some food as you pelted out of the house, show him what you have and approach slowly.
- If you have nerves of steel, make sure that your Pom can see you and then you run away, as if playing a game. He will most likely follow you.

If you've run out of the house, called and called your buddy, and he is still nowhere to be found, start Plan B. Every dog owner should have at least 20 lost dog posters made up and ready to go at all times. Each poster should include:

- A large picture of a Pom (this doesn't have to be your dog but should be the same general shape and color) with a very large "LOST DOG" headline. Remember that most people will see the poster from their car.
- Information on whether your dog is microchipped and needs medication. This lets anyone who might have picked him up know that you can positively identify him as yours and that he may need extensive and expensive medical care. They don't need to know that the "medication" is your Pom's monthly heartworm preventive.
- Your telephone number so that you can easily be reached should someone locate your dog.

If your Pom is lost during the day, try to get these posters out within the hour. If lost at night, try to have them out by first daylight. Then fax or scan and e-mail the posters to all of the vets in your area. Call your local animal control to let the staff know what's going on, and follow their instructions. Call the local police as well—some will accept lost dog data. Follow up every couple of days.

2. Drive around the block.
3. Continue going on longer and longer rides to fun places like the dog park until he is comfortable in the car.

PET-FRIENDLY LODGING

These days, we are in the midst of a revolution of dog friendliness. As more and people demand services for their four-legged companions, more and more individual hotels accept dogs, as do some hotel chains.

But freedom brings responsibility. Consider yourself an ambassador for all dog lovers, and treat your hotel not just like your own comfortable home but like persnickety Aunt Mildred's—you know, where everything is always spotless.

Follow these rules scrupulously:

• Always pick up after your dog, and potty him only in the hotel's designated areas.

When staying in a hotel or motel with your Pom, put a blanket on the bed to keep it free of dog hair.

Your Pom is the consummate companion and partner.

• Unless you are absolutely one hundred percent sure that your Pom will not potty inside, keep him in his crate at all times in your room. If loose, only have him in a belly band (male) or britches (female). Many dogs who are absolutely housetrained at home are not so on the road because their schedule and space have been altered.

• Carry your Pom through all public areas. Even the best-mannered dog can make a mistake in a strange place. Once they need to go, most dogs are not used to walking for several minutes before they can relieve themselves.

• If you must leave your buddy alone in your room, keep him in his crate with the door closed and covered, as this will show him that he is off-duty and can relax. If your Pom insists on barking, you will need to respect the other guests and take him with you. Perhaps the concierge can hook you up with a local doggy daycare where you can leave your Pom for a few hours.

Your Pom can be your companion and partner. Most Pom owners, once smitten, swear they will never have another breed. Bred to be the ultimate companion, Pomeranians are a cheerful sidekick to any escapade. And how hard can life be, accompanied by a cheerful and happy-go-lucky Pom? Maybe not so hard after all.

RESOURCES

ASSOCIATIONS AND ORGANIZATIONS

BREED CLUBS

American Kennel Club (AKC)
8051 Arco Corporate Drive,
Suite 100
Raleigh, NC 27617-3390
Telephone: (919) 233-9767
Fax: (919) 233-3627
E-Mail: info@akc.org
www.akc.org

American Pomeranian Club (APC)
www.americanpomeranianclub.org

Canadian Kennel Club (CKC)
200 Ronson Drive, Suite 400
Etobicoke, Ontario M9W 5Z9
Telephone: (416) 675-5511
Fax: (416) 675-6506
E-Mail: information@ckc.ca
www.ckc.ca

Fédération Cynologique Internationale (FCI)
FCI Office
Place Albert 1er, 13
B – 6530 Thuin
Belgique
Telephone: +32 71 59.12.38
Fax: +32 71 59.22.29
www.fci.be

The Kennel Club
1-5 Clarges Street, Piccadilly,
London W1J 8AB
Telephone: 0844 463 3980
Fax: 020 7518 1028
www.thekennelclub.org.uk

The Pomeranian Club UK
http://thepomeranianclubuk.
weebly.com

United Kennel Club (UKC)
100 E. Kilgore Road
Kalamazoo, MI 49002-5584
Telephone: (269) 343-9020
Fax: (269) 343-7037
www.ukcdogs.com

PET SITTERS

National Association of Professional Pet Sitters (NAPPS)
15000 Commerce Parkway, Suite C
Mt. Laurel, New Jersey 08054
Telephone: (856) 439-0324
Fax: (856) 439-0525
E-Mail: napps@petsitters.org
www.petsitters.org

Pet Sitters International
201 East King Street
King, NC 27021-9161
Telephone: (336) 983-9222
Fax: (336) 983-5266
E-Mail: info@petsit.com
www.petsit.com

RESCUE ORGANIZATIONS AND ANIMAL WELFARE GROUPS

American Humane Association
1400 16th Street NW, Suite 360
Washington, DC 20036
Telephone: (800) 227-4645
E-Mail: info@americanhumane.org
www.americanhumane.org

American Society for the Prevention of Cruelty to Animals (ASPCA)
424 E. 92nd Street
New York, NY 10128-6804
Telephone: (212) 876-7700
www.aspca.org

Royal Society for the Prevention of Cruelty to Animals (RSPCA)
RSPCA Advice Team
Wilberforce Way
Southwater
Horsham
West Sussex
RH13 9RS
United Kingdom
Telephone: 0300 1234 999
www.rspca.org.uk

SPORTS

International Agility Link (IAL)
85 Blackwall Road
Chuwar, Queensland
Australia 4306
Telephone: 61 (07) 3202 2361
Fax: 61 (07) 3281 6872
Email: steve@agilityclick.com
www.agilityclick.com/~ial/

The North American Dog Agility Council (NADAC)
24605 Dodds Rd.
Bend, Oregon 97701
www.nadac.com

North American Flyball Association (NAFA)
1333 West Devon Avenue, #512
Chicago, IL 60660
Telephone: (800) 318-6312
Fax: (800) 318-6312
Email: flyball@flyball.org
www.flyball.org

United States Dog Agility Association (USDAA)
P.O. Box 850955
Richardson, TX 75085
Telephone: (972) 487-2200
Fax: (972) 231-9700
www.usdaa.com

The World Canine Freestyle Organization, Inc.
P.O. Box 350122
Brooklyn, NY 11235
Telephone: (718) 332-8336
Fax: (718) 646-2686
E-Mail: WCFODOGS@aol.com
www.worldcaninefreestyle.org

THERAPY
Pet Partners
875 124th Ave, NE, Suite 101
Bellevue, WA 98005
Telephone: (425) 679-5500
Fax: (425) 679-5539
E-Mail: info@petpartners.org
www.petpartners.org

Therapy Dogs Inc.
P.O. Box 20227
Cheyenne, WY 82003
Telephone: (877) 843-7364
Fax: (307) 638-2079
E-Mail: therapydogsinc@
qwestoffice.net
www.therapydogs.com

Therapy Dogs International (TDI)
88 Bartley Road
Flanders, NJ 07836
Telephone: (973) 252-9800
Fax: (973) 252-7171
E-Mail: tdi@gti.net
www.tdi-dog.org

TRAINING
American College of Veterinary Behaviorists (ACVB)
College of Veterinary Medicine,
4474 TAMU
Texas A&M University
College Station, Texas 77843-4474
www.dacvb.org

American Kennel Club Canine Health Foundation, Inc. (CHF)
P. O. Box 900061
Raleigh, NC 27675
Telephone: (888) 682-9696
Fax: (919) 334-4011
www.akcchf.org

Association of Professional Dog Trainers (APDT)
104 South Calhoun Street
Greenville, SC 29601
Telephone: (800) PET-DOGS
Fax: (864) 331-0767
E-Mail: information@apdt.com
www.apdt.com

International Association of Animal Behavior Consultants (IAABC)
565 Callery Road
Cranberry Township, PA 16066
E-Mail: info@iaabc.org
www.iaabc.org

National Association of Dog Obedience Instructors (NADOI)
7910 Picador Drive
Houston, TX 77083-4918
Telephone: (972) 296-1196
E-Mail: info@nadoi.org
www.nadoi.org

VETERINARY AND HEALTH RESOURCES
The Academy of Veterinary Homeopathy (AVH)
P. O. Box 232282
Leucadia, CA 92023-2282
Telephone: (866) 652-1590
Fax: (866) 652-1590
www.theavh.org

American Academy of Veterinary Acupuncture (AAVA)
P.O. Box 1058
Glastonbury, CT 06033
Telephone: (860) 632-9911
www.aava.org

American Animal Hospital Association (AAHA)
12575 W. Bayaud Ave.
Lakewood, CO 80228
Telephone: (303) 986-2800
Fax: (303) 986-1700
E-Mail: info@aahanet.org
www.aahanet.org

American College of Veterinary Internal Medicine (ACVIM)
1997 Wadsworth Blvd., Suite A
Lakewood, CO 80214-5293
Telephone: 303-231-9933
Telephone (US or Canada): (800) 245-9081
Fax: (303) 231-0880
Email: ACVIM@ACVIM.org
www.acvim.org

American College of Veterinary Ophthalmologists (ACVO)
P.O. Box 1311
Meridian, ID 83860
Telephone: (208) 466-7624
Fax: (208) 466-7693
E-Mail: office13@acvo.com
www.acvo.org

American Heartworm Society (AHS)
P.O. Box 8266
Wilmington, DE 19803-8266
Email: info@heartwormsociety.org
www.heartwormsociety.org

American Holistic Veterinary Medical Association (AHVMA)
P. O. Box 630
Abingdon, MD 21009-0630
Telephone: (410) 569-0795
Fax: (410) 569-2346
E-Mail: office@ahvma.org
www.ahvma.org

American Veterinary Medical Association (AVMA)
1931 North Meacham Road, Suite 100
Schaumburg, IL 60173-4360
Telephone: (800) 248-2862
Fax: (847) 925-1329
www.avma.org

ASPCA Animal Poison Control Center
Telephone: (888) 426-4435
www.aspca.org

British Veterinary Association (BVA)
7 Mansfield Street
London
W1G 9NQ
Telephone: 020 7636 6541
Fax: 020 7908 6349
E-Mail: bvahq@bva.co.uk
www.bva.co.uk

Canine Eye Registration Foundation (CERF)
P.O. Box 199
Rantoul, Il 61866-0199
Telephone: (217) 693-4800
Fax: (217) 693-4801
E-Mail: CERF@vmdb.org
www.vmdb.org

Orthopedic Foundation for Animals (OFA)
2300 E. Nifong Boulevard
Columbia, MO 65201-3806
Telephone: (573) 442-0418
Fax: (573) 875-5073
Email: ofa@offa.org
www.offa.org

US Food and Drug Administration Center for Veterinary Medicine (CVM)
7519 Standish Place
HFV-12
Rockville, MD 20855
Telephone: (240) 276-9300
Email: AskCVM@fda.hhs.gov
www.fda.gov/AnimalVeterinary/

PUBLICATIONS

BOOKS

Anderson, Teoti. *The Super Simple Guide to Housetraining.* Neptune City: TFH Publications, 2004.

Anne, Jonna, with Mary Straus. *The Healthy Dog Cookbook: 50 Nutritious and Delicious Recipes Your Dog Will Love.* UK: Ivy Press Limited, 2008.

Grant, Lexiann. Terra-Nova *The Pomeranian.* TFH Publications, Inc., 2006.

Stocker, Marguerite. Animal Planet *Pomeranians.* TFH Publications, Inc., 2006.

MAGAZINES
AKC Family Dog
American Kennel Club
260 Madison Avenue
New York, NY 10016
Telephone: (800) 490-5675
E-Mail: familydog@akc.org
www.akc.org/pubs/familydog

AKC Gazette : Digital Edition
American Kennel Club
260 Madison Avenue
New York, NY 10016
www.akc.org/pubs/gazette/digital_edition.cfm

WEBSITES
Nylabone
www.nylabone.com

TFH Publications, Inc.
www.tfh.com

INDEX

Note: **Boldfaced** numbers indicate illustrations.

PHOTO CREDITS

ACKNOWLEDGMENTS

Several Pomeranian breeders and owners assisted me with their insight and stories for this book. I loved the story from Carol Kingsley about Tito chasing the rabbit into its warren and then getting stuck. I can just see him underground, curled up and calmly waiting for his rescue. Catherine Murphy, DVM, my vet and longtime small dog specialist, side-checked the health chapter. I also must mention my mentor, Karen Huey, as much of the information in the training and grooming chapters originated with her.

To my embarrassment, I have to admit I have never met my editor, Stephanie Fornino of TFH, in person. She has been kind and helpful. Her pithy editing notes, like the classic "Not really sure what this means..." served well to puncture my wilder flights of fancy, reducing them to clear and understandable prose.

I want to also mention my husband, George. Yes, he is the unpaid kennel help and pill giver extraordinaire, an uncomplaining helper willing to take care of the dogs when I am on the road. More importantly, he has supported me steadfastly in all my endeavors over the last 36 years of marriage. This book is dedicated to him.

However, although the data stemmed in large part from others, any mistakes in Dogs 101 Animal Planet *Pomeranian* lie solely with me.

So please—enjoy! I hope you have as much fun in reading this book as I had fun in writing it.

ABOUT THE AUTHOR

Sandy Bergstrom Mesmer grew up in West Hartford, Connecticut. She attended her first dog show when she was eight and fell instantly in love with all the different breeds and the atmosphere of knowledge and purpose—not to mention the faint odor of hair spray.

Fast forward 16 years and Sandy bought her first show dog, a Yorkshire Terrier named Robbie of Badhadlan. He was her constant buddy and companion and introduced her to the fun and challenge of showing dogs. She has been breeding and showing Silky Terriers since 1981, completing more than 92 home-bred champions, including several top winners.

Sandy is trained as a pastoral counselor affiliated with the Church of Scientology. She founded Jefferson Academy, a private K through 8 school, and was headmistress there for ten years. In 1994 she left the school and joined the Mace Kingsley Family Center, where she has worked ever since. She currently travels all over the world, working with families and their children. Sandy began writing in 2000, publishing her first book, *How to Turn Your Dog into a Show-Off*, in 2002. She is also a Maxwell Award-winning artist. Her training advice and artwork can be found on her website, www. about-small-dogs.com.

Sandy fell in love with Pomeranians when she met her boss Carol's rescue Pom, Tito. Hearing the great stories about the intrepid Tito inspired her to write this book.

ABOUT ANIMAL PLANET™

Animal Planet™ is the only television network dedicated exclusively to the connection between humans and animals. The network brings people of all ages together by tapping into our fundamental fascination with animals through an array of fresh programming that includes humor, competition, drama, and spectacle from the animal kingdom.

ABOUT *DOGS 101*

The most comprehensive—and most endearing—dog encyclopedia on television, *DOGS 101* spotlights the adorable, the feisty and the unexpected. A wide-ranging rundown of everyone's favorite dog breeds—from the Dalmatian to Xoloitzcuintli—this series surveys a variety of breeds for their behavioral quirks, genetic history, most famous examples and wildest trivia. Learn which dogs are best for urban living and which would be the best fit for your family. Using a mix of animal experts, pop-culture footage and stylized dog photography, *DOGS 101* is an unprecedented look at man's best friend.

At Animal Planet, we're committed to providing quality products designed to help your pets live long, healthy, and happy lives.